ABOUT IDG BOOKS WORLDWIDE

Welcome to the world of IDG Books Worldwide.

IDG Books Worldwide, Inc., is a subsidiary of International Data Group, the world's largest publisher of computer-related information and the leading global provider of information services on information technology. IDG was founded more than 30 years ago by Patrick J. McGovern and now employs more than 9,000 people worldwide. IDG publishes more than 290 computer publications in over 75 countries. More than 90 million people read one or more IDG publications each month.

Launched in 1990, IDG Books Worldwide is today the #1 publisher of best-selling computer books in the United States. We are proud to have received eight awards from the Computer Press Association in recognition of editorial excellence and three from Computer Currents' First Annual Readers' Choice Awards. Our best-selling ...For Dummies® series has more than 50 million copies in print with translations in 31 languages. IDG Books Worldwide, through a joint venture with IDG's Hi-Tech Beijing, became the first U.S. publisher to publish a computer book in the People's Republic of China. In record time, IDG Books Worldwide has become the first choice for millions of readers around the world who want to learn how to better manage their businesses.

Our mission is simple: Every one of our books is designed to bring extra value and skill-building instructions to the reader. Our books are written by experts who understand and care about our readers. The knowledge base of our editorial staff comes from years of experience in publishing, education, and journalism — experience we use to produce books to carry us into the new millennium. In short, we care about books, so we attract the best people. We devote special attention to details such as audience, interior design, use of icons, and illustrations. And because we use an efficient process of authoring, editing, and desktop publishing our books electronically, we can spend more time ensuring superior content and less time on the technicalities of making books.

You can count on our commitment to deliver high-quality books at competitive prices on topics you want to read about. At IDG Books Worldwide, we continue in the IDG tradition of delivering quality for more than 30 years. You'll find no better book on a subject than one from IDG Books Worldwide.

John Kilcullen
Chairman and CEO
IDG Books Worldwide, Inc.

VIII
WINNER
Eighth Annual
Computer Press
Awards >1992

IX
WINNER
Ninth Annual
Computer Press
Awards >1993

X
WINNER
Tenth Annual
Computer Press
Awards >1994

XI
WINNER
Eleventh Annual
Computer Press
Awards >1995

maranGraphics is a family-run business located near Toronto, Canada.

At **maranGraphics**, we believe in producing great computer books–one book at a time.

Each maranGraphics book uses the award-winning communication process that we have been developing over the last 25 years. Using this process, we organize screen shots, text and illustrations in a way that makes it easy for you to learn new concepts and tasks.

We spend hours deciding the best way to perform each task, so you don't have to! Our clear, easy-to-follow screen shots and instructions walk you through each task from beginning to end.

Our detailed illustrations go hand-in-hand with the text to help reinforce the information. Each illustration is a labor of love–some take up to a week to draw!

We want to thank you for purchasing what we feel are the best computer books money can buy. We hope you enjoy using this book as much as we enjoyed creating it!

Sincerely,

The Maran Family

Please visit us on the Web at:
www.maran.com

Credits

Author:
Ruth Maran

Technical Consultant:
Paul Whitehead

Copy Editors:
Raquel Scott
Jill Maran
Roxanne Van Damme

Project Manager:
Judy Maran

Editors:
Janice Boyer
Stacey Morrison

Screen Captures:
James Menzies

Layout Designer:
Treena Lees

Illustrators:
Russ Marini
Sean Johannesen
Steven Schaerer
Ted Sheppard

Screen Artist & Illustrator:
Jimmy Tam

Indexer:
Janice Boyer

Post Production:
Robert Maran

**Senior Vice President,
Technology Publishing
IDG Books Worldwide:**
Richard Swadley

**Editorial Support
IDG Books Worldwide:**
Barry Pruett
Martine Edwards

Acknowledgments

Thanks to the dedicated staff of maranGraphics, including
Jennifer Amaral, Cathy Benn, Janice Boyer, Sean Johannesen,
Eric Kramer, Usha Krishnan, Wanda Lawrie, Treena Lees,
Jill Maran, Judy Maran, Robert Maran, Sherry Maran,
Russ Marini, James Menzies, Stacey Morrison, Teri Lynn Pinsent,
Steven Schaerer, Raquel Scott, Ted Sheppard, Jimmy Tam,
Roxanne Van Damme, Paul Whitehead and Kelleigh Wing.

Finally, to Richard Maran who originated the easy-to-use
graphic format of this guide. Thank you for your
inspiration and guidance.

Table of Contents

CHAPTER

EDIT TEXT

CHAPTER

FORMAT WEB PAGES

CHAPTER

ADD IMAGES

Table of Contents

CHAPTER 9

CHAPTER 1

GETTING STARTED

Are you thinking about creating Web pages? This chapter will help you get started.

FrontPage allows you to create, edit, manage and publish Web pages.

EDIT AND FORMAT TEXT

FrontPage offers many features that help you edit and format text on your Web pages. You can add, delete and rearrange text as well as check your Web pages for spelling errors. You can enhance or emphasize information by using various fonts, styles and colors or apply a theme to instantly give your Web pages a professional look.

ADD IMAGES

You can add images to illustrate concepts or enhance the appearance of your Web pages. You can add images such as drawings, paintings, photographs, charts and diagrams. FrontPage offers many ways to enhance images, such as adding a border to an image.

CREATE LINKS

You can create links to connect a word, phrase or image on a Web page to another page in your own Web site or on the Web. You can also create links that readers can select to send you an e-mail message, play a sound or play a video.

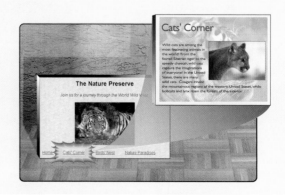

CREATE TABLES

You can create a table to neatly display a list of information on a Web page. Tables are also useful for controlling the placement of text and images on a Web page.

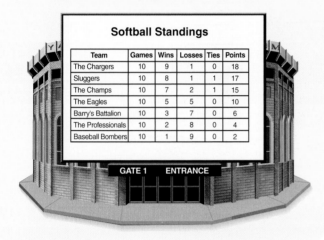

CREATE FRAMES

You can create frames to divide a Web browser window into sections. Each section will display a different Web page. Frames allow you to display information such as a company logo or navigational tools that will remain on the screen while readers browse through your Web pages.

CREATE FORMS

Forms allow you to gather information from readers who visit your Web pages. You can create forms that let readers send you questions or comments about your Web pages. You can also create forms that allow readers to purchase your products and services on the Web.

PUBLISH WEB PAGES

When you finish creating your Web pages, FrontPage helps you transfer the pages to a Web server to make the pages available on the Web. Web servers are computers on the Internet that store, monitor and control access to Web pages.

The World Wide Web is part of the Internet and consists of a huge collection of documents stored on computers around the world.

The World Wide Web is also called the Web.

Web Server

A Web server is a computer that stores Web pages and makes the pages available on the Web for other people to view.

Web Site

A Web site is a collection of Web pages created and maintained by a college, university, government agency, company, organization or individual.

Web Page

A Web page is a document on the Web. Web pages can include text, images, sound and video.

URL

Each Web page has a unique address, called a Uniform Resource Locator (URL). You can display any Web page if you know its URL.

LINKS

Web pages contain links, which are highlighted text or images on a Web page that connect to other pages on the Web. You can select a link to display a Web page located on the same computer or on a computer across the city, country or world.

Links allow you to easily navigate through a vast amount of information by jumping from one Web page to another. Links are also known as hyperlinks.

WEB BROWSERS

A Web browser is a program that allows you to view and explore information on the Web.

Microsoft Internet Explorer

Microsoft Internet Explorer is a popular Web browser that comes with the latest versions of Windows. You can also obtain Microsoft Internet Explorer at the www.microsoft.com/windows/ie Web site.

Netscape Navigator

Netscape Navigator is a popular Web browser that you can obtain at the www.netscape.com Web site or at computer stores.

HTML

HyperText Markup Language (HTML) is a computer language used to create Web pages. Web pages are HTML documents that consist of text and special instructions called tags. A Web browser interprets the tags in an HTML document and displays the document as a Web page. FrontPage hides the tags when you create a Web page.

REASONS FOR CREATING WEB PAGES

PERSONAL

SHARE PERSONAL INFORMATION

Many people create Web pages to share information about their families, pets, vacations or favorite hobbies. Some people create Web pages to present a résumé to potential employers.

SHARE KNOWLEDGE

Many scientists and business professionals make their work available on the Web. If you are experienced in an area that many people want to learn more about, you can create Web pages to share your knowledge.

ENTERTAIN READERS

Many people create Web pages to display collections of jokes or humorous stories. You can also create Web pages to display information, pictures, sound clips and videos about a favorite celebrity, sports team or TV show.

PROMOTE INTERESTS

You can create Web pages to display information about an organization or club that you belong to. You can include a schedule of upcoming events and detailed information about the goals of the organization.

COMMERCIAL

PROVIDE INFORMATION

Companies often place pages on the Web to provide information about their business and the products and services they offer. Companies can use Web pages to keep the public informed about new products and interesting news. Many companies display their press releases on the Web.

SHOPPING

Many companies create Web pages that allow readers to order products and services over the Internet. Companies can display descriptions and pictures of products to help readers determine which products they want to purchase.

JOB LISTINGS

Many companies use Web pages to advertise jobs that are available within the company. Some companies allow readers to submit résumés on their Web sites.

CONTACT INFORMATION

Companies can display their office addresses, e-mail addresses and phone numbers on their Web pages. This helps readers contact the company to ask questions and express opinions.

WEB PAGE CONTENT CONSIDERATIONS

PROOFREAD INFORMATION

Carefully check your Web pages for spelling and grammar errors. Spelling mistakes can make readers think that the information on your Web pages is inaccurate. You may want to print your Web pages to help you proofread the pages.

PUT IMPORTANT INFORMATION FIRST

Always display the most important information at the top of each Web page. Some readers may not scroll through a Web page to read all the information. These readers will miss important information if you do not display the information at the top of the page.

PAGE LENGTH

Web pages should not be too short or too long. If a Web page is shorter than half a screen of information, try to combine the information with another page. If a Web page is longer than five screens, try to break up the page into several shorter pages.

PROVIDE A FAQ

A FAQ is a list of Frequently Asked Questions about a topic. A FAQ can help answer questions that people have about your Web pages and can help prevent people from sending you e-mail messages asking the same questions repeatedly.

COPYRIGHT CONSIDERATIONS

If you plan to use information or images you did not create, make sure the information or images are not copyrighted. Many pages on the Web offer information and images that do not have copyright restrictions.

UPDATE INFORMATION

You should update your Web pages on a regular basis. If the information on your Web pages never changes, people may read the pages only once and may not revisit them in the future. You should include the date on your Web pages to let readers know when you last updated the pages.

TRANSFER SPEED

When creating your Web pages, try to keep the file size of the pages and images as small as possible. This will speed up the display of your Web pages by reducing the time it takes for the information to transfer.

INCLUDE CONTACT INFORMATION

Always include your name and e-mail address on Web pages you create. This allows readers to contact you if they have questions or comments.

The home page is the main Web page in a Web site. The home page is the first page people will see when they visit a Web site.

When you create a Web site, FrontPage automatically names your home page index.htm.

SUMMARY

Always include a brief summary of your Web pages on your home page. You should state the purpose of your Web pages, such as whether you want to entertain or inform readers. You should not assume that readers will understand the purpose of your Web pages just by reading the title.

TABLE OF CONTENTS

Your home page can include a table of contents that lists the information contained in your Web site. You can include links that allow readers to quickly access information of interest.

BOOKMARK REMINDER

Web browsers have a feature called bookmarks or favorites that allows people to store the addresses of Web pages they visit. You can include an image or phrase on your home page to remind readers to bookmark your Web page. This allows readers to quickly return to your Web site.

A mouse is a handheld device that lets you select and move items on your screen.

When you move the mouse on your desk, the mouse pointer on your screen moves in the same direction. The mouse pointer assumes different shapes, such as $\&$ or I, depending on its location on your screen and the task you are performing.

Resting your hand on the mouse, use your thumb and two rightmost fingers to move the mouse on your desk. Use your two remaining fingers to press the mouse buttons.

MOUSE ACTIONS

Click

Press and release the left mouse button.

Double-click

Quickly press and release the left mouse button twice.

Right-click

Press and release the right mouse button.

Drag

Position the mouse pointer ($\&$) over an object on your screen and then press and hold down the left mouse button as you move the mouse to where you want to place the object. Then release the button.

You can start FrontPage to create Web pages that you can publish on the Web.

START FRONTPAGE

1 Click **Start**.

2 Click **Programs**.

3 Click **Microsoft FrontPage**.

■ The Microsoft FrontPage window appears.

The FrontPage window displays many items to help you use FrontPage.

WEB SITE NAME

Shows the location and name of the displayed Web site.

MENU BAR

Provides access to lists of commands available in FrontPage.

STANDARD TOOLBAR

Contains buttons to help you select common commands, such as Save and Print.

FORMATTING TOOLBAR

Contains buttons to help you select common formatting commands, such as Bold and Italic.

WEB PAGE NAME

Shows the name of the displayed Web page.

VIEWS BAR

Provides access to six different views of your Web site that you can use to create and organize your Web pages.

PAGE VIEW TABS

Provides access to three different views of your Web page.

SCROLL BARS

Allow you to browse through a Web page.

ESTIMATED DOWNLOAD TIME

Indicates how many seconds the displayed Web page will take to transfer to a reader's computer when using a 28.8 Kb/s modem.

FrontPage offers several toolbars that you can display or hide at any time. Each toolbar contains buttons that help you quickly perform common tasks.

When you first start FrontPage, the Standard and Formatting toolbars appear on your screen.

Standard

Formatting

DISPLAY OR HIDE A TOOLBAR

1 Click **View**.

2 Click **Toolbars**.

■ A list of toolbars appears. A check mark (✔) beside a toolbar name tells you the toolbar is currently displayed.

3 Click the name of the toolbar you want to display or hide.

■ FrontPage displays or hides the toolbar you selected.

Note: A screen displaying fewer toolbars provides a larger and less cluttered working area.

When you finish using FrontPage, you can exit the program.

You should always exit FrontPage and all other programs before turning off your computer.

EXIT FRONTPAGE

■ Before exiting FrontPage, you should save all the Web pages in your Web site. To save a Web page, see page 30.

1 Click ⌧ to exit FrontPage.

■ The Microsoft FrontPage window disappears from your screen.

■ If you have more than one Web site open, you need to repeat step **1** for each Web site.

If you do not know how to perform a task in FrontPage, you can search for help information on the task.

GETTING HELP

1 Click 🖻 to get help information on a specific task.

■ The Microsoft FrontPage Help window appears.

2 Click the **Answer Wizard** tab.

3 To select the text in this area, drag the mouse I over the text until you highlight all the text.

4 Type your question and then press the **Enter** key.

TIP

Why *do some words in the* Microsoft FrontPage Help window appear blue and underlined?

Words or phrases that appear blue and underlined are links that will display help topics related to the help information you are currently viewing. To display a related help topic, click the highlighted word or phrase.

What do you want to do?

Learn more about publishing

Publish a web using HTTP

Publish a web using FTP

Publish a web to a file system location

TIP

How can I determine the *function of a toolbar button?*

When you position the mouse over a button on a toolbar, the name of the button appears in a yellow box. This information can help you determine what task the button allows you to perform.

■ A list of help topics related to your question appears in this area.

5 Click a help topic of interest.

■ Information about the help topic you selected appears in this area.

6 When you finish reviewing the help information, click ☒ to close the Microsoft FrontPage Help window.

CHAPTER 2

FRONTPAGE BASICS

Are you ready to begin creating your Web pages? This chapter will provide you with the basics you need to get started.

You can use a template or wizard to create a new Web site. Templates and wizards provide the layout and design for your Web site.

Template
A template provides areas for you to fill in your personalized information.

Wizard
A wizard asks you a series of questions and then uses your answers to create a Web site.

A Web site is a collection of Web pages.

CREATE A NEW WEB SITE

1 Click ▾ in this area.

2 Click **Web** to create a new Web site.

■ The New dialog box appears.

3 Click the template or wizard you want to use to create a new Web site.

Note: The icon for a wizard displays a magic wand (✶✎).

■ This area displays a description of the template or wizard you selected.

How can I create a blank Web site?

You can use one of the following templates to create a blank Web site. A blank Web site gives you the most flexibility and control.

The **One Page Web** template creates a Web site containing one blank Web page.

The **Empty Web** template creates an empty Web site that contains no Web pages. You can add the Web pages you need.

 Where will FrontPage store my Web sites?

When you installed FrontPage on your computer, a folder called "My Webs" was automatically created in the My Documents folder. FrontPage stores your Web sites in this folder.

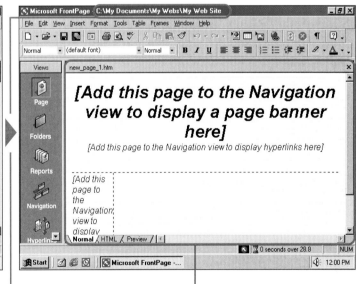

■ This area displays the location where FrontPage will store the Web site on your computer and the name of the Web site.

4 To change the name of the Web site, drag the mouse I over the existing name and then type a new name.

5 Click **OK** to create the Web site.

■ FrontPage creates the Web site.

Note: If you selected a wizard in step 3, FrontPage will ask you a series of questions before creating the Web site.

■ This area displays the location and name of the Web site.

■ This area displays a page in the Web site. You can add your personalized information to the appropriate areas to complete each Web page.

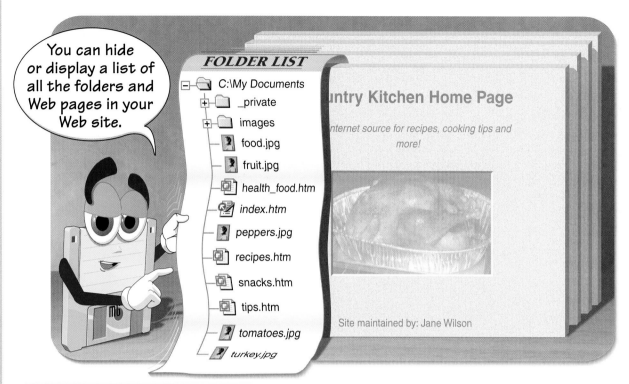

You can hide or display a list of all the folders and Web pages in your Web site.

FOLDER LIST

- C:\My Documents
  - _private
  - images
  - food.jpg
  - fruit.jpg
  - health_food.htm
  - index.htm
  - peppers.jpg
  - recipes.htm
  - snacks.htm
  - tips.htm
  - tomatoes.jpg
  - turkey.jpg

...untry Kitchen Home Page

...nternet source for recipes, cooking tips and more!

Site maintained by: Jane Wilson

Hiding the Folder List will give you a larger and less cluttered working area.

HIDE OR DISPLAY THE FOLDER LIST

■ The Folder List appears automatically when you create a Web site.

■ The Folder List displays all the folders (📁) and Web pages (📄) in your Web site.

1 Click 📧 to hide the Folder List.

■ The Folder List disappears.

■ To once again display the Folder List, click 📧.

24

FrontPage allows you to type text into your Web page quickly and easily.

My Home Page

ENTER TEXT

■ The text you type will appear where the insertion point flashes on your screen.

1 Type the text you want to display on your Web page.

Note: In this book, the font of text was changed to Arial to make the Web page examples easier to read. To change the font of text, see page 68.

■ When the text you type reaches the end of a line, FrontPage automatically wraps the text to the next line. You need to press the Enter key only when you want to start a new paragraph.

■ FrontPage automatically underlines misspelled words in red. The underlines will not appear when you publish your Web page. To correct misspelled words, see page 60.

When typing the text on your Web page, you can specify where you want a new line of text to begin.

Starting a new line of text is useful for separating short lines of text, such as text in a mailing address or poem.

START A NEW LINE OF TEXT

1 Click the location where you want to start a new line of text without creating a new paragraph.

2 Press and hold down the **Shift** key as you press the **Enter** key.

■ The flashing insertion point appears on the next line. You can now type the text you want to appear on the new line.

*Note: When you start a new line of text, no space appears between the lines. When you use only the **Enter** key, a blank line appears between the lines of text.*

26

> You can add a blank Web page to discuss a new topic in your Web site.

CREATE A BLANK WEB PAGE

1 Click ☐ to create a blank Web page.

■ A blank Web page appears.

■ This area displays a temporary name for the Web page. To save and name the Web page, see page 30.

■ You can immediately add information to the Web page.

You can use a template to save time when creating a new Web page. A template provides you with the layout and design for a Web page.

CREATE A WEB PAGE USING A TEMPLATE

1 Click **File**.

2 Click **New**.

3 Click **Page**.

■ The New dialog box appears.

4 Click the **General** tab.

■ This area displays the templates you can use to create your Web page.

5 Click the template you want to use.

TIP

Why would I use a template to create a new Web page?

If you are new to creating Web pages, templates can provide a good starting point for the layout and design of your Web pages. Templates also provide sample text that can help you determine what text you should include on your Web pages. You can replace the sample text with your own personalized information. FrontPage offers a variety of templates, such as a bibliography, feedback form, guest book and table of contents.

■ A description of the template appears in this area.

■ A preview of the template appears in this area.

6 Click **OK** to create the Web page.

*Note: If you selected **Form Page Wizard** in step 5, FrontPage will ask you a series of questions before creating the Web page.*

■ The Web page appears.

■ This area displays a temporary name for the Web page. To save and name the Web page, see page 30.

7 Add your personalized information to the appropriate areas to complete the Web page. You can replace the existing text and images with your own information.

You should save your Web page to store the page for future use. This lets you later review and edit the Web page.

If your Web page contains images, FrontPage will ask you to save the images when you save the Web page.

You should regularly save changes you make to a Web page to avoid losing your work.

SAVE A WEB PAGE

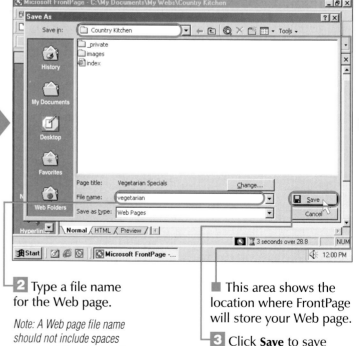

1 Click 🖫 to save your Web page.

■ The Save As dialog box appears.

Note: If you previously saved the Web page, the Save As dialog box will not appear since you have already named the page.

2 Type a file name for the Web page.

*Note: A Web page file name should not include spaces or unusual characters, such as * or #.*

■ This area shows the location where FrontPage will store your Web page.

3 Click **Save** to save the Web page.

Where will FrontPage store a Web page on my computer?

When you installed FrontPage on your computer, a folder called "My Webs" was automatically created in the My Documents folder. The My Webs folder contains a separate folder for each Web site you create. FrontPage will store a new Web page in the folder for the current Web site.

When I save a Web page, why do I need to save the images displayed on the page?

When you add an image to a Web page, you must save the image as part of your Web site. A copy of the image will be stored in the same folder that stores all the Web pages for your Web site. This ensures the image will transfer with your Web site when you publish your Web pages.

■ If your Web page displays images you have not yet saved, the Save Embedded Files dialog box appears.

■ This area lists the images displayed on the Web page.

■ This area displays a preview of the first image in the list.

4 Click **OK** to save the images with your Web site.

■ FrontPage saves your Web page and the images displayed on the page.

■ This area displays the name of the Web page.

You can open a Web site you previously saved. This allows you to review and make changes to the Web site.

OPEN A WEB SITE

1 Click ⬝ in this area.

2 Click **Open Web**.

■ The Open Web dialog box appears.

■ This area shows the location of the displayed folders.

3 To display a list of your Web sites, click 🔼 to display the contents of the My Webs folder.

Note: FrontPage automatically stores your Web sites in the My Webs folder.

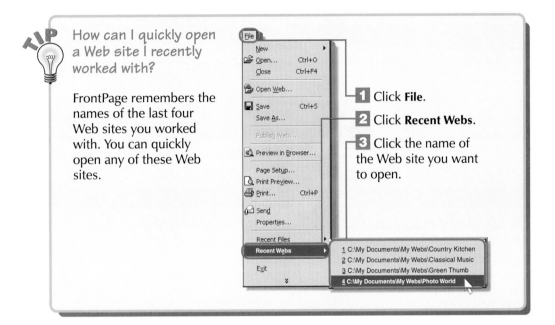

TIP

How can I quickly open a Web site I recently worked with?

FrontPage remembers the names of the last four Web sites you worked with. You can quickly open any of these Web sites.

-1 Click **File**.

-2 Click **Recent Webs**.

-3 Click the name of the Web site you want to open.

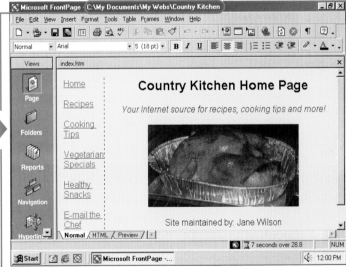

-4 Click the name of the Web site you want to open.

-5 Click **Open** to open the Web site.

■ The Web site opens and appears on your screen. You can now review and make changes to the Web pages in the Web site.

■ This area displays the location and name of the Web site.

Note: If you already had a Web site open, the Web site you open will appear in a different FrontPage window.

CHAPTER 3

WORK WITH WEB PAGES

Would you like to work effectively with your Web pages? This chapter shows you how to print, rename, delete Web pages and more.

You can use the scroll bar to browse through the information on your Web page.

SCROLL THROUGH A WEB PAGE

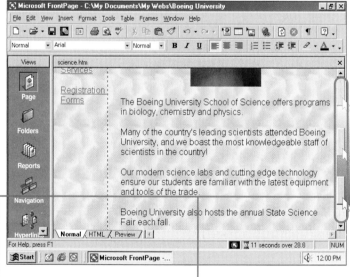

SCROLL DOWN

1 To scroll down one line, click ▼.

SCROLL UP

1 To scroll up one line, click ▲.

SCROLL TO ANY POSITION

1 Drag the scroll box along the scroll bar until the information you want to view appears.

■ The location of the scroll box indicates which part of the Web page you are viewing. To view the middle of the Web page, drag the scroll box halfway down the scroll bar.

You can produce a paper copy of the Web page displayed on your screen. This is useful for reviewing and editing the Web page.

Before printing your Web page, make sure your printer is turned on and contains paper.

PRINT A WEB PAGE

1 Click **File**.

2 Click **Print**.

■ The Print dialog box appears.

3 Click the print option you want to use (○ changes to ⊙).

All
Prints every page of the Web page.

Pages
Prints the pages you specify.

4 If you selected **Pages** in step **3**, type the first page you want to print. Press the **Tab** key and then type the last page you want to print.

5 Click **OK**.

You can easily switch between the Web pages in your Web site. This allows you to review and edit more than one Web page at a time.

USING THE FOLDER LIST

■ This area displays all the Web pages (▦) in your Web site.

■ If the list does not appear, click ▦ to display the list.

1 Double-click the Web page you want to display.

■ This area displays the contents of the Web page you selected. You can now review and edit the Web page.

■ This area displays the name of the Web page.

What is the difference between the way the Folder List and the Window menu display Web pages?

Folder List

✔ Displays all the Web pages in your Web site.

✔ Displays only the Web pages you have saved.

✔ A pencil (✎) appears in the icon for Web pages that are currently open.

Window Menu

✔ Displays up to nine Web pages that are currently open in your Web site.

✔ Displays saved and unsaved Web pages.

✔ A star (*) appears beside Web pages that you have changed but have not yet saved.

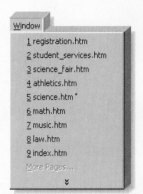

USING THE WINDOW MENU

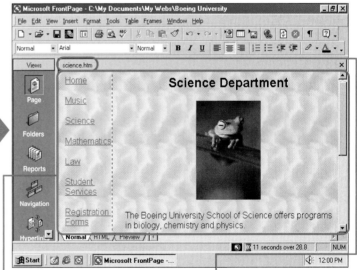

1 Click **Window** to display a list of Web pages that are currently open in your Web site.

■ The Web page you are currently working with appears at the top of the list.

2 Click the Web page you want to display.

■ This area displays the contents of the Web page you selected. You can now review and edit the Web page.

■ This area displays the name of the Web page.

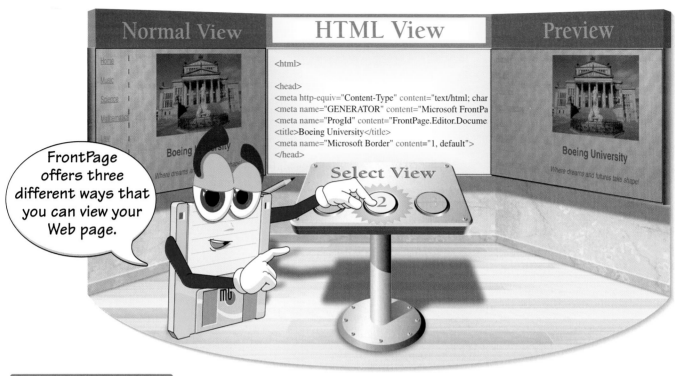

FrontPage offers three different ways that you can view your Web page.

USING THE PAGE VIEWS

■ By default, the Web page appears in the Normal view.

1 Click a tab to display the Web page in a different view.

NORMAL

■ The Normal view allows you to enter, edit and format the information on your Web page.

TIP

How are HTML tags used to create a Web page?

Each tag gives a specific instruction and is surrounded by angle brackets < >. Most tags have an opening tag and a closing tag that affect the text between the tags. The closing tag has a forward slash (/). Some tags have only an opening tag. Here are some common tags.

Tag	Description
<b>	Bolds text
<blockquote>	Separates a section of text from the main text
<body>	Identifies the main content of a Web page
<i>	Italicizes text
<p>	Starts a new paragraph
<title>	Creates a title for a Web page

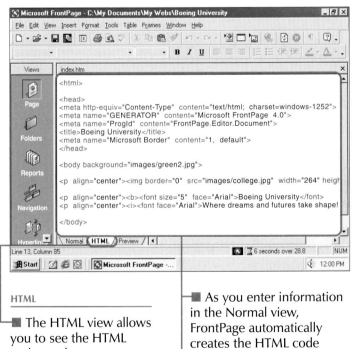

HTML

■ The HTML view allows you to see the HTML code used to create your Web page.

■ As you enter information in the Normal view, FrontPage automatically creates the HTML code for the Web page.

■ HTML code consists of text and special instructions called tags. Each tag is shown in blue.

PREVIEW

■ The Preview view allows you to see how your Web page will appear on the Web.

Note: The Preview view is available only if you have the Microsoft Internet Explorer Web browser installed on your computer.

You can display your Web page in a Web browser to see how the page will appear on the Web.

A Web browser is a program that allows you to view and explore information on the Web.

DISPLAY A WEB PAGE IN A WEB BROWSER

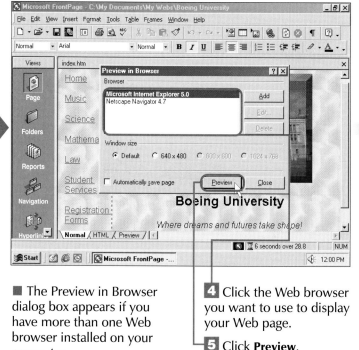

1 Click 🖫 to save any changes you made to your Web page.

Note: For information on saving a Web page, see page 30.

2 Click **File**.

3 Click **Preview in Browser**.

■ The Preview in Browser dialog box appears if you have more than one Web browser installed on your computer.

4 Click the Web browser you want to use to display your Web page.

5 Click **Preview**.

Should I display my Web page in more than one Web browser?

You should display your Web page in several Web browsers so you can see how each browser will display your Web page. Each Web browser will display your Web page in a slightly different way. The most popular Web browsers are Microsoft Internet Explorer and Netscape Navigator.

Microsoft Internet Explorer

Microsoft Internet Explorer comes with the latest versions of Windows. You can also obtain Internet Explorer at the www.microsoft.com/windows/ie Web page.

Netscape Navigator

You can obtain Netscape Navigator at the www.netscape.com Web site or at computer stores.

■ The Web browser opens and displays the Web page.

6 When you finish reviewing the Web page, click **X** to close the Web browser window.

QUICKLY DISPLAY A WEB PAGE IN A WEB BROWSER

1 Click 🔍 to quickly display a Web page in a Web browser.

■ The Web page will appear in the Web browser you last used to display a Web page.

FrontPage offers six different views of your Web site that you can use to create and organize your Web pages.

CHANGE THE VIEW OF A WEB SITE

■ When you first start FrontPage, your Web site appears in the Page view.

1 To change the view, click the icon for the view you want to use.

■ You can click ▼ to browse through the views.

■ Your Web site appears in the view you selected.

THE WEB SITE VIEWS

PAGE

The Page view allows you to enter, edit and format the information on your Web pages.

FOLDERS

The Folders view displays the folder structure of your Web site and lists information about the Web pages, images and other files in your Web site.

REPORTS

The Reports view allows you to display various reports that analyze and summarize information about your Web site.

NAVIGATION

The Navigation view allows you to view and work with the navigational structure of the Web pages in your Web site.

HYPERLINKS

The Hyperlinks view allows you to view the links that connect each Web page to other pages in your Web site.

TASKS

The Tasks view allows you to create a to-do list to keep track of tasks you need to accomplish to complete your Web site.

You can use the Folders view to display information about the Web pages, images and other files in your Web site.

FOLDERS VIEW

USING THE FOLDERS VIEW

1 Click **Folders** to display your Web site in the Folders view.

■ This area displays the folders in your Web site.

2 Click a folder to display the contents of the folder.

Note: To display all the files in your Web site, click the top folder.

■ This area displays the contents of the folder you selected. FrontPage displays information about the Web pages (📄), images (🖼) and other files in your Web site.

■ To view the files in a different order, click the heading of the column you want to use to sort the files.

Note: You can click the heading of the column again to sort the files in the opposite order.

You can give a Web page a title that describes the contents of the page. The title appears at the top of a Web browser window.

If you do not specify a title for your Web page, FrontPage will use the first line of text as your title.

You should use a brief, descriptive title that will interest people in reading your Web page. Use a title such as "Favorite Golf Getaways" rather than a less descriptive title such as "My Home Page."

CHANGE THE TITLE OF A WEB PAGE

1 Click the Web page you want to change.

2 Click **File**.

3 Click **Properties**.

Note: If Properties does not appear on the menu, position the mouse ⬚ over the bottom of the menu to display all the menu commands.

■ The Properties dialog box appears.

4 Type a title for the Web page.

5 Click **OK** to confirm the information you entered.

■ When a reader displays the Web page, the title will appear at the top of the Web browser window. To preview a Web page in a Web browser, see page 42.

You can rename a Web page to better describe the contents of the page.

You should not rename the Web page named index.htm since this is your home page. If you rename this Web page, readers may get an error message when they visit your Web site.

RENAME A WEB PAGE

■ This area displays all the folders (📁) and Web pages (📄) in your Web site.

■ If the list does not appear, click 🔲 to display the list.

1 Click the name of the Web page you want to rename.

2 Wait a moment and then click the name of the Web page again.

■ The name of the Web page appears in a box.

3 Type a new name for the Web page and then press the **Enter** key. Make sure you add the **.htm** extension to the end of the Web page name.

*Note: A dialog box will appear if the Web page is linked to other Web pages in your Web site. Click **Yes** to have FrontPage automatically update the linked pages.*

48

You can delete a Web page you no longer want to include in your Web site.

Before you delete any Web pages, consider the value of your work. Do not delete a Web page unless you are certain you no longer need the page.

You should not delete the Web page named index.htm since this is your home page. If you delete this Web page, readers may get an error message when they visit your Web site.

DELETE A WEB PAGE

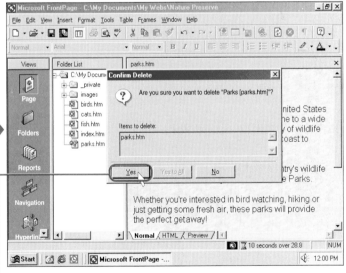

■ This area displays all the folders (🗀) and Web pages (🗐) in your Web site.

■ If the list does not appear, click 🖽 to display the list.

1 Click the name of the Web page you want to delete.

2 Press the `Delete` key.

■ A confirmation dialog box appears.

3 Click **Yes** to delete the Web page.

■ FrontPage deletes the Web page.

CHAPTER 4

EDIT TEXT

Are you wondering how to edit the text on your Web pages or check your pages for spelling errors? This chapter explains how.

e endless!

•FrontPage•
Thesaurus

LINCOLN
BOOKS

Before performing many tasks in FrontPage, you must select the text you want to work with. Selected text appears highlighted on your screen.

journey

SELECT TEXT

SELECT A WORD

1 Double-click the word you want to select.

■ To deselect text, click outside the selected area.

SELECT ANY AMOUNT OF TEXT

1 Position the mouse I to the left of the first word you want to select.

2 Drag the mouse I over the text until you highlight all the text you want to select.

FrontPage remembers the last changes you made to your Web page. If you regret these changes, you can cancel them by using the Undo feature.

The Undo feature can cancel up to 30 of your last editing and formatting changes.

UNDO CHANGES

1 Click to undo the last change you made to your Web page.

■ FrontPage cancels the last change you made to your Web page.

■ You can repeat step 1 to cancel previous changes you made.

■ To reverse the results of using the Undo feature, click .

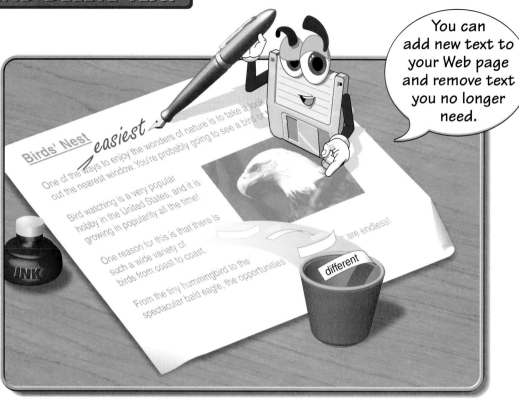

You can add new text to your Web page and remove text you no longer need.

INSERT TEXT

1 Click the location where you want to insert the new text.

■ The text you type will appear where the insertion point flashes on your screen.

Note: You can press the ←, →, ↑ or ↓ key to move the insertion point.

2 Type the text you want to insert. To insert a blank space, press the **Spacebar**.

■ The words to the right of the new text move forward.

TIP

How can I easily enter numbers on my Web page?

When **NUM** appears at the bottom of your screen, you can use the number keys on the right side of your keyboard to enter numbers. To turn the display of **NUM** on or off, press the `Num Lock` key.

TIP

How can I use the keyboard to quickly move the insertion point?

To move the insertion point	Press
To the end of a line	`End`
To the beginning of a line	`Home`
To the end of a paragraph	Ctrl and `↓` at the same time
To the beginning of a paragraph	Ctrl and `↑` at the same time
One screen down	`Page Down`
One screen up	`Page Up`

DELETE TEXT

1 Select the text you want to delete. To select text, see page 52.

2 Press the `Delete` key to remove the text.

■ The text disappears. The remaining text moves to fill the empty space.

■ To delete a single character, click to the right of the character you want to delete and then press the `←Backspace` key. FrontPage deletes the character to the left of the flashing insertion point.

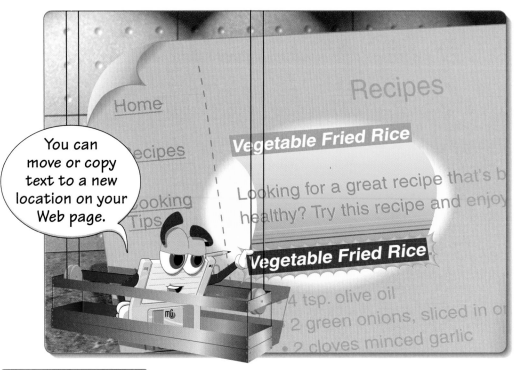

You can move or copy text to a new location on your Web page.

Moving text allows you to rearrange text on your Web page. When you move text, the text disappears from its original location.

Copying text allows you to repeat information on your Web page without having to retype the text. When you copy text, the text appears in both the original and new locations.

MOVE OR COPY TEXT

USING DRAG AND DROP

1 Select the text you want to move. To select text, see page 52.

2 Position the mouse I over the selected text (I changes to).

3 To move the text, drag the mouse to where you want to place the text.

Note: The text will appear where you position the dotted insertion point on your screen.

■ The text moves to the new location.

■ To copy text, perform steps 1 to 3, except press and hold down the Ctrl key as you perform step 3.

56

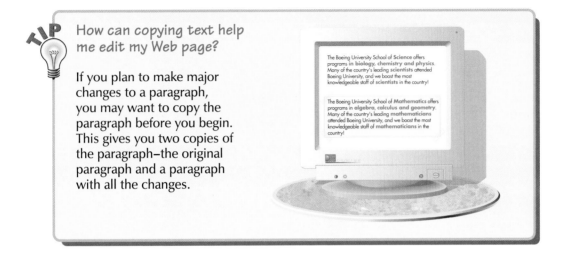

TIP

How can copying text help me edit my Web page?

If you plan to make major changes to a paragraph, you may want to copy the paragraph before you begin. This gives you two copies of the paragraph–the original paragraph and a paragraph with all the changes.

USING THE TOOLBAR BUTTONS

1 Select the text you want to move or copy. To select text, see page 52.

2 Click one of the following buttons.

✂ Move text

📋 Copy text

3 Click the location where you want to place the text.

4 Click 📋 to place the text in the new location.

■ The text appears in the new location.

You can insert symbols or special characters that do not appear on your keyboard into your Web page.

INSERT SYMBOLS

1 Click the location where you want a symbol to appear on your Web page.

2 Click **Insert**.

3 Click **Symbol**.

Note: If Symbol does not appear on the menu, position the mouse ⟲ over the bottom of the menu to display all the menu commands.

■ The Symbol dialog box appears.

4 Click the symbol you want to place on your Web page.

■ An enlarged version of the symbol appears in this area.

How can I quickly add a symbol to many locations on my Web page?

After you insert a symbol, you can copy the symbol to various locations on your Web page. This is useful if you need to insert a symbol such as ™ next to each instance of your company name. For information on copying text, see page 56.

5 Click **Insert** to insert the symbol into your Web page.

6 Click **Close** to close the Symbol dialog box.

■ The symbol appears on your Web page.

■ To remove a symbol from a Web page, drag the mouse I over the symbol to select the symbol. Then press the Delete key.

You can quickly find and correct all the spelling errors on your Web page.

CHECK SPELLING

■ FrontPage automatically checks your Web page for spelling errors as you type. Misspelled words display a red, wavy underline. The underlines will not appear when you publish your Web page.

1 Click 📝 to start the spell check.

■ The Spelling dialog box appears if FrontPage finds a misspelled word on your Web page.

■ This area displays the misspelled word.

■ This area displays suggestions for correcting the word.

TIP

How does FrontPage find spelling errors on my Web page?

FrontPage compares every word on your Web page to words in its own dictionary. If a word does not exist in the dictionary, the word is considered misspelled.

FrontPage will not find a correctly spelled word used in the wrong context, such as "My niece is **sit** years old." You should carefully reread your Web page to find this type of error.

2 Click the word you want to use to correct the misspelled word.

3 Click **Change** to replace the word on your Web page with the word you selected.

■ To skip the word and continue checking your Web page, click **Ignore**.

*Note: To skip the word and all other occurrences of the word on your Web page, click **Ignore All**.*

4 Change or ignore misspelled words until this dialog box appears, telling you the spell check is complete.

5 Click **OK** to close the dialog box.

You can use the thesaurus to replace a word on your Web page with a word that is more suitable.

Word

Suggestions

BIG LARGE HUGE IMMENSE GIGANTIC

USING THE THESAURUS

1 Click the word you want to replace with another word.

2 Click **Tools**.

3 Click **Thesaurus**.

Note: If Thesaurus does not appear on the menu, position the mouse over the bottom of the menu to display all the menu commands.

■ The Thesaurus dialog box appears.

4 Click the most appropriate meaning of the word.

■ This area displays words that share the meaning you selected.

How can the thesaurus help me?

Many people use the thesaurus to replace a word that appears repeatedly on a Web page. Replacing repeatedly used words can help add variety to your writing. Using the thesaurus included with FrontPage is faster and more convenient than searching through a printed thesaurus.

5 Click the word you want to use on your Web page.

6 Click **Replace** to replace the word on your Web page with the word you selected.

■ If the thesaurus does not offer a suitable replacement for the word, click **Cancel** to close the Thesaurus dialog box.

■ The word you selected replaces the word on your Web page.

■ To deselect text, click outside the selected area.

CHAPTER 5

FORMAT WEB PAGES

Are you wondering how to change the appearance of text on your Web pages? Read this chapter to learn how.

BOLD, ITALICIZE OR UNDERLINE TEXT

You can bold, italicize or underline text to emphasize information on your Web page.

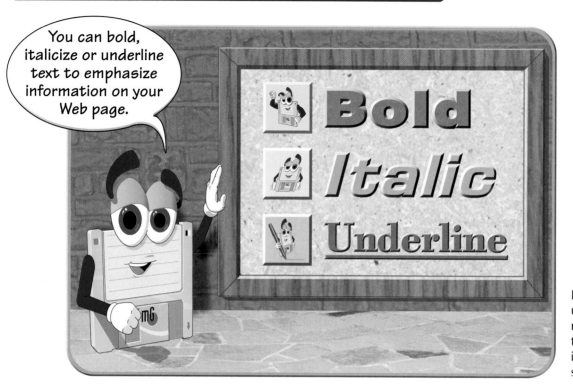

Be careful when underlining text, since readers may think the text is a link. For information on links, see pages 114 to 133.

BOLD, ITALICIZE OR UNDERLINE TEXT

1 Select the text you want to change to a new style. To select text, see page 52.

2 Click one of the following options.

B Bold

I Italic

U Underline

■ The text you selected appears in the new style.

■ To deselect text, click outside the selected area.

■ To remove a bold, italic or underline style, repeat steps 1 and 2.

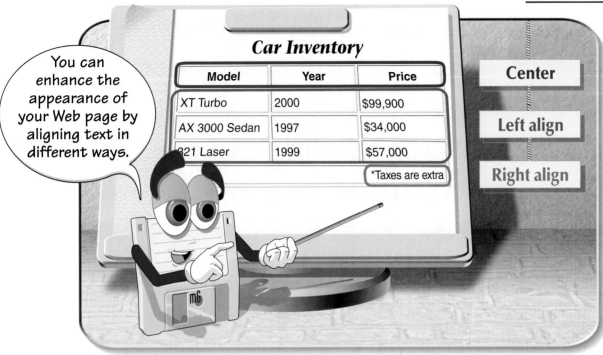

You can enhance the appearance of your Web page by aligning text in different ways.

CHANGE ALIGNMENT OF TEXT

1 Select the text you want to align differently. To select text, see page 52.

2 Click one of the following options.

≣ Left align

≣ Center

≣ Right align

■ The text appears in the new alignment.

■ To deselect text, click outside the selected area.

Beethoven

Ludwig van Beethoven was born in Bonn, Germany in 1770. He spent most of his life giving concerts, teaching piano and selling his compositions.

Bach

Johann Sebastian ___ was born into a ___ of musicians ___ in Eisenach, Germany ___ Bach's w___ include church organ and ch___ music ___ or chamber orchestras and o___ 200 cantatas.

Monotype Corsiva

You can change the font of text to enhance the appearance of your Web page.

You should choose common fonts for your Web page, such as Arial or Times New Roman. If a font you choose is not available on a reader's computer, the Web browser will use a different font and your text may not appear the way you expected.

CHANGE FONT OF TEXT

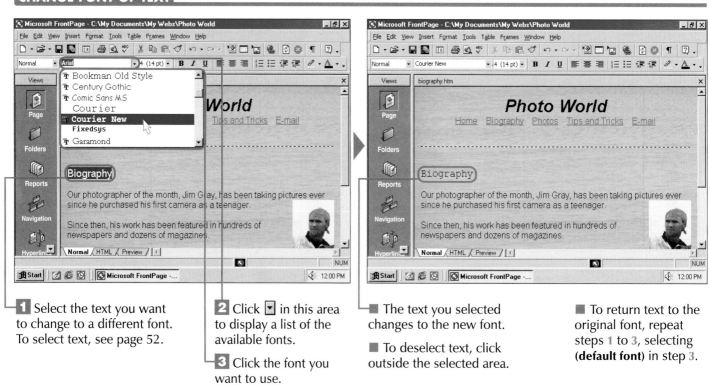

1 Select the text you want to change to a different font. To select text, see page 52.

2 Click ▼ in this area to display a list of the available fonts.

3 Click the font you want to use.

■ The text you selected changes to the new font.

■ To deselect text, click outside the selected area.

■ To return text to the original font, repeat steps **1** to **3**, selecting **(default font)** in step **3**.

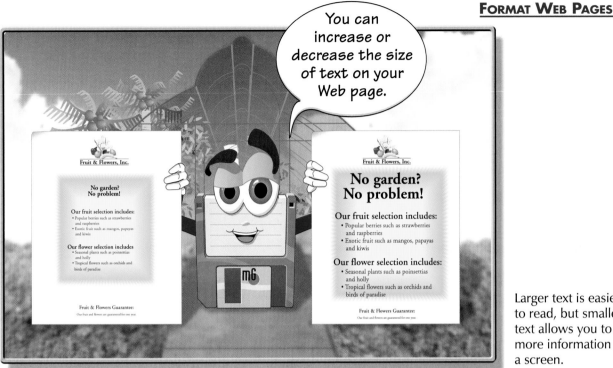

You can increase or decrease the size of text on your Web page.

Larger text is easier to read, but smaller text allows you to fit more information on a screen.

CHANGE SIZE OF TEXT

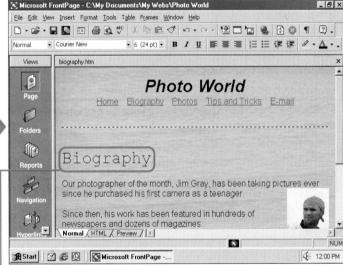

1 Select the text you want to change to a new size. To select text, see page 52.

2 Click this area to display a list of the available sizes.

3 Click the size you want to use.

■ The text you selected changes to the new size.

■ To deselect text, click outside the selected area.

■ To return text to the original size, repeat steps **1** to **3**, selecting **Normal** in step **3**.

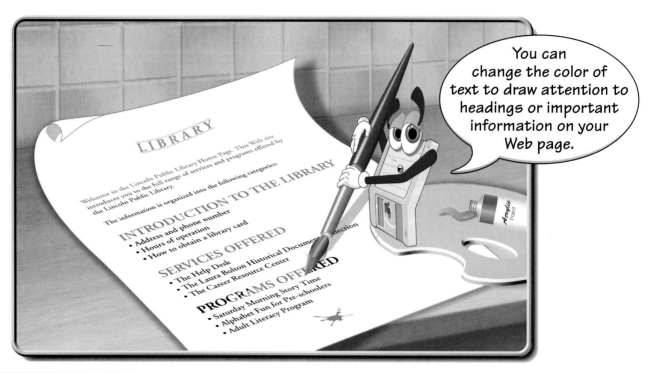

You can change the color of text to draw attention to headings or important information on your Web page.

CHANGE COLOR OF TEXT

1 Select the text you want to change to a different color. To select text, see page 52.

2 Click ▾ in this area to display the available colors.

3 Click the color you want to use.

■ The text appears in the color you selected.

■ To deselect text, click outside the selected area.

■ To return text to its original color, repeat steps **1** to **3**, selecting **Automatic** in step **3**.

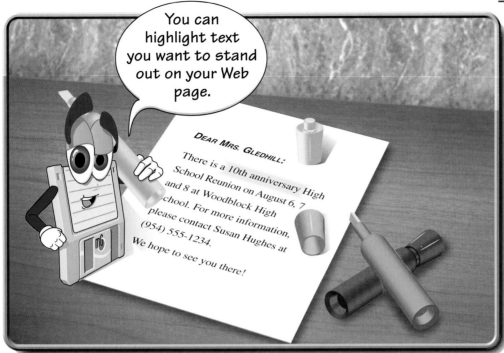

Highlighting text is also useful for marking information you want to review or verify later.

HIGHLIGHT TEXT

1 Select the text you want to highlight. To select text, see page 52.

2 Click ⦙ in this area to display the available highlight colors.

3 Click the highlight color you want to use.

■ The text appears highlighted in the color you selected.

■ To deselect text, click outside the selected area.

■ To remove a highlight, repeat steps **1** to **3**, selecting **Automatic** in step **3**.

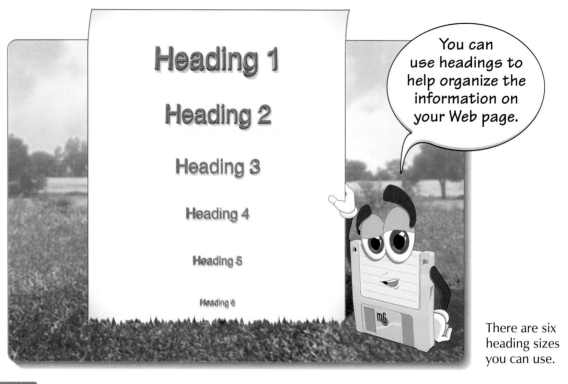

You can use headings to help organize the information on your Web page.

There are six heading sizes you can use.

1 Select the text you want to make a heading. To select text, see page 52.

2 Click this area to display a list of the available headings.

3 Click the heading size you want to use.

■ The text appears as a heading on your Web page.

■ To deselect text, click outside the selected area.

■ To remove the heading formatting from text, repeat steps **1** to **3**, selecting **Normal** in step **3**.

HEADING CONSIDERATIONS

PROVIDE AN OUTLINE

You can use headings to provide an outline of the Web page for your readers. By scanning the headings, a reader should get a general overview of the information covered on the Web page and be able to quickly locate topics of interest.

USE HEADINGS CONSISTENTLY

Make sure you use headings consistently on a Web page to help readers understand the relative importance of information. Use the same heading size for all headings of equal importance.

PROPER USE OF HEADINGS

Use headings to signify the importance of information on your Web page. Do not use headings to add a certain look or style to text. Since different Web browsers display headings in slightly different ways, you cannot predict exactly how a heading will look to readers.

SUBHEADINGS

When creating subheadings, do not skip heading sizes. For example, a size 2 heading should be followed by a size 3 subheading.

You can make one area of text on your Web page look exactly like another.

COPY FORMATTING

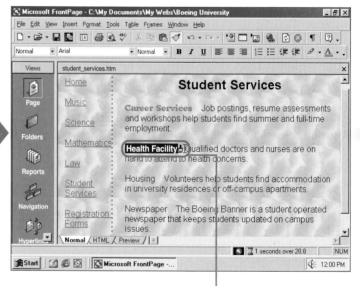

1 Select the text that displays the formatting you want to copy. To select text, see page 52.

2 Click ✍ to copy the formatting.

■ The mouse ▷ changes to ▴Ⅰ when over your Web page.

3 Select the text you want to display the same formatting.

Why would I want to copy the formatting of text?

You may want to copy the formatting of text to make all the headings or important words on your Web page look the same. This will give your Web page a consistent appearance.

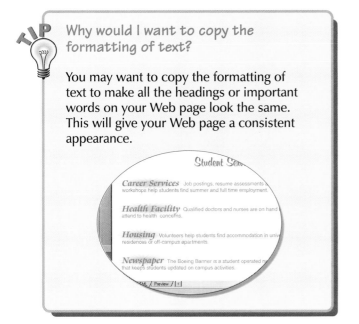

Can I copy the formatting of a link?

You can copy the formatting of a link to another word or phrase on your Web page. The text you copy the formatting to will link to the same destination as the original text.

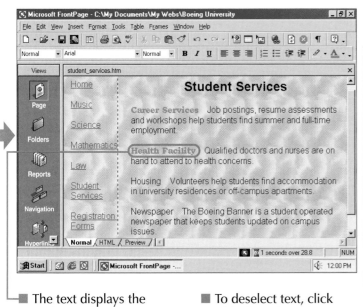

■ The text displays the same formatting.

■ To deselect text, click outside the selected area.

COPY FORMATTING TO SEVERAL AREAS

1 Select the text that displays the formatting you want to copy. To select text, see page 52.

2 Double-click to copy the formatting.

3 Select each area of text you want to display the same formatting.

4 When you finish selecting each area of text, press the **Esc** key.

You can indent text to make paragraphs on your Web page stand out.

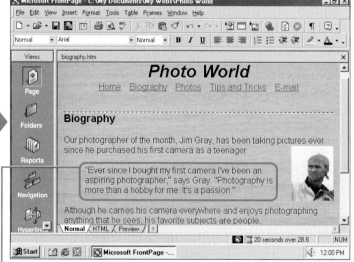

1 Select the text you want to indent. To select text, see page 52.

2 Click one of the following buttons.

⏴ Decrease indent

⏵ Increase indent

■ FrontPage indents the text you selected from both sides of the Web page.

■ You can repeat step 2 to further indent the text.

■ To deselect text, click outside the selected area.

You can create a definition list to display terms and their definitions. This type of list is ideal for a glossary.

CREATE A DEFINITION LIST

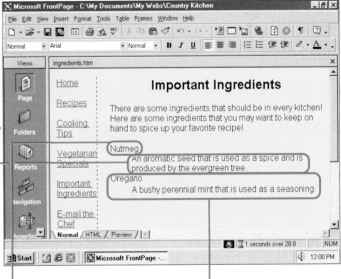

1 Click the location where you want the first term to appear.

2 Click this area to display a list of styles.

3 Click **Defined Term**.

Note: You may need to scroll through the list to display the Defined Term option. To use the scroll bar, see page 36.

4 Type the first term in the list and then press the Enter key.

■ FrontPage automatically adds an indent for the definition of the term.

5 Type the definition of the term and then press the Enter key.

6 Repeat steps 4 and 5 for each term you want to include in the list.

■ When you complete the list, press the Enter key twice.

> You can separate items in a list by beginning each item with a bullet or number.

CREATE A BULLETED OR NUMBERED LIST

1 Select the text you want to display bullets or numbers. To select text, see page 52.

2 Click **Format**.

3 Click **Bullets and Numbering**.

■ The Bullets and Numbering dialog box appears.

4 Click the tab for the type of list you want to create.

5 Click the style you want to use.

6 Click **OK** to confirm your selection.

TIP

What type of list should I create?

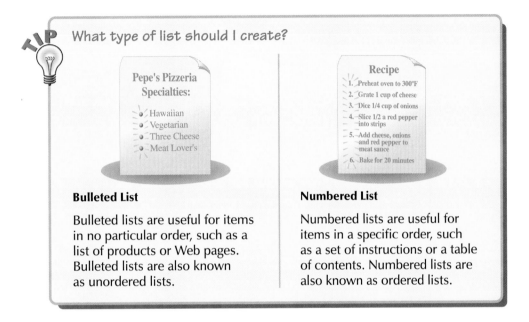

Bulleted List

Bulleted lists are useful for items in no particular order, such as a list of products or Web pages. Bulleted lists are also known as unordered lists.

Numbered List

Numbered lists are useful for items in a specific order, such as a set of instructions or a table of contents. Numbered lists are also known as ordered lists.

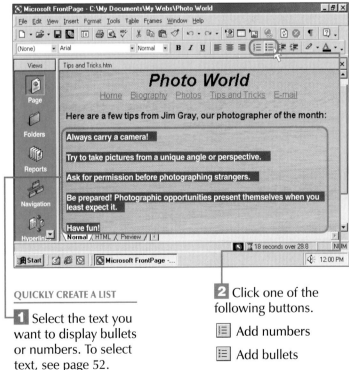

■ A bullet or number appears in front of each item in the list.

■ To deselect text, click outside the selected area.

■ To remove bullets or numbers from a list, repeat steps **1** to **6**, selecting the top left style in step **5**.

QUICKLY CREATE A LIST

1 Select the text you want to display bullets or numbers. To select text, see page 52.

2 Click one of the following buttons.

▤ Add numbers

▤ Add bullets

CHANGE BACKGROUND COLOR

1 Click **Format**.

2 Click **Background**.

Note: If Background does not appear on the menu, position the mouse ⅄ over the bottom of the menu to display all the menu commands.

■ The Page Properties dialog box appears.

■ This area displays the current background color of your Web page.

TIP

What should I consider when changing the background color of my Web page?

Make sure you select a background color that works well with the color of your text. For example, red text on a blue background can be difficult to read. To help the readability of the text on your Web page, try to use dark text on a light background or light text on a dark background. To change text color, see page 70.

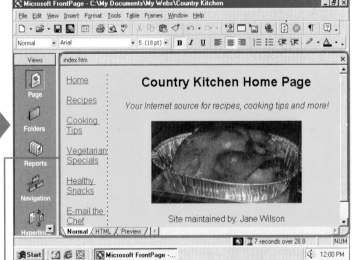

3 Click this area to select a new background color for your Web page.

4 Click the background color you want to use.

5 Click **OK** to confirm your selection.

■ The Web page background displays the color you selected.

■ To return to the original background color, repeat steps **1** to **5**, selecting **Automatic** in step **4**.

FrontPage offers many themes that you can choose from to give your Web pages a professional appearance.

A theme will change the way fonts, colors, bullets and lines appear on your Web pages.

APPLY A THEME

1 Click **Format**.

2 Click **Theme**.

■ The Themes dialog box appears.

3 Click an option to apply the theme to all the pages in your Web site or just the current page (○ changes to ⦿).

4 Click the theme you want to use.

■ This area displays a sample of the theme you selected.

Note: You can repeat step 4 to view a sample of a different theme.

5 Click **OK** to apply the selected theme.

TIP

How can I change the appearance of a theme?

In the Themes dialog box, FrontPage provides additional options you can use to customize themes. You can click an option to turn the option on (☑) or off (☐).

Vivid colors

Use brighter colors.

Active graphics

Use animated graphics.

Background picture

Use a background image.

■ A dialog box may appear, stating that applying a theme will change the appearance of your Web pages and replace some of the formatting changes you previously made.

6 Click **Yes** to continue.

■ The Web page(s) you specified display the theme.

■ To remove a theme from Web pages, repeat steps **1** to **6**, selecting **[No Theme]** in step **4**.

BIRD WATCHERS' HOME PAGE

The page dedicated to people who love to watch birds!

Bird watchers appreciate the beauty and wonder of birds, and this month, with summer just around the corner, we will discuss the best spots for birdwatching in the national parks of the northern states. These locations have all been recommended by visitors to our page. If you have a new location to add, please e-mail us today!

Popular Sites

Membership
Information

ership
ation

CHAPTER 6

ADD IMAGES

Would you like to add images to your Web pages? This chapter shows you how.

REASONS FOR USING IMAGES

GRAPHICS

You can add images to your Web pages to display drawings, paintings and computer-generated art. You can also add images that help illustrate a concept that is difficult to explain with words. For example, you can include a map to give directions, a chart to show financial trends or a diagram to point out essential parts of a product.

PHOTOGRAPHS

You can display photographs of your family, pets or favorite celebrities on your Web pages. Many companies include photographs of their products so people around the world can view the products without having to visit a store or wait for a brochure to arrive in the mail.

TYPES OF IMAGES

When you save a Web page that contains an image, FrontPage automatically converts the image to the GIF or JPEG format. The GIF and JPEG formats are the most popular image formats on the Web.

GIF

Graphics Interchange Format (GIF) images are limited to 256 colors and are often used for logos, banners and computer-generated art. GIF images have the .gif extension (example: logo.gif).

JPEG

Joint Photographic Experts Group (JPEG) images can have millions of colors and are often used for photographs and very large images. JPEG images have the .jpg extension (example: stonehenge.jpg).

OBTAIN IMAGES

INTERNET

Many Web sites offer images you can use free of charge on your Web pages. Make sure you have permission to use any images you obtain on the Web. You can find images at the following Web sites:

www.allfree-clipart.com

www.bestclipart.com/photographs/photoframes.htm

www.noeticart.com

SCAN IMAGES

You can use a scanner to scan images into your computer. You can scan photographs, logos and drawings and then place the scanned images on your Web pages. If you do not have a scanner, many service bureaus will scan images for a fee.

CREATE IMAGES

You can use an image editing program to create your own images. Creating your own images lets you design images that best suit your Web pages. Popular image editing programs include Adobe Photoshop and Paint Shop Pro.

IMAGE COLLECTIONS

You can buy collections of ready-made images at computer stores. Image collections can include cartoons, drawings, photographs or computer-generated art.

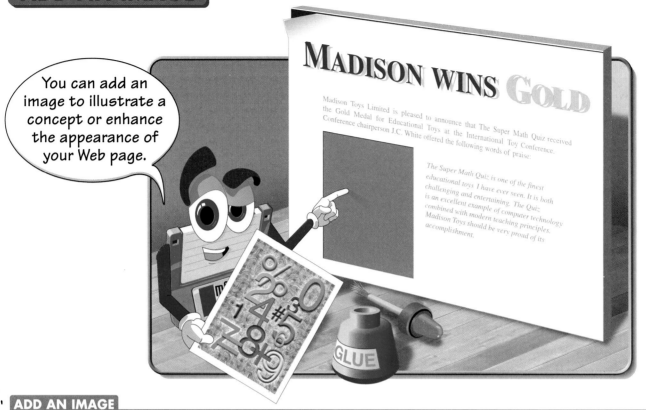

You can add an image to illustrate a concept or enhance the appearance of your Web page.

MADISON WINS GOLD

Madison Toys Limited is pleased to announce that The Super Math Quiz received the Gold Medal for Educational Toys at the International Toy Conference. Conference chairperson J.C. White offered the following words of praise:

The Super Math Quiz is one of the finest educational toys I have ever seen. It is both challenging and entertaining. The Quiz is an excellent example of computer technology combined with modern teaching principles. Madison Toys should be very proud of its accomplishment.

ADD AN IMAGE

1 Click the location where you want to add an image to your Web page.

2 Click 🖼 to add an image.

■ The Picture dialog box appears.

3 Click 🔍 to locate the image on your computer that you want to use.

■ This area displays images you have previously added to your Web site. To add one of these images, click the image. Then press the **Enter** key to add the image.

What should I consider when adding an image to a Web page?

View Web Pages Without Images

Make sure your Web pages will
look attractive and make sense if
the images are not displayed. Some
readers turn off the display of images
to browse the Web more quickly,
while others use Web browsers
that cannot display images.

Image Size

Images increase the time it takes for
a Web page to appear on a screen.
If a Web page takes too long to appear,
readers may lose interest and move to
another page. Whenever possible, you
should use images with small file sizes
since these images will transfer faster.

■ The Select File dialog
box appears.

■ This area shows the
location of the displayed
files. You can click this area
to change the location.

4 Click the image you
want to appear on your
Web page.

5 Click **OK** to confirm
your selection.

■ The image appears
on your Web page.

*Note: To move or resize an
image, see page 92.*

■ To delete an image,
click the image and then
press the Delete key.

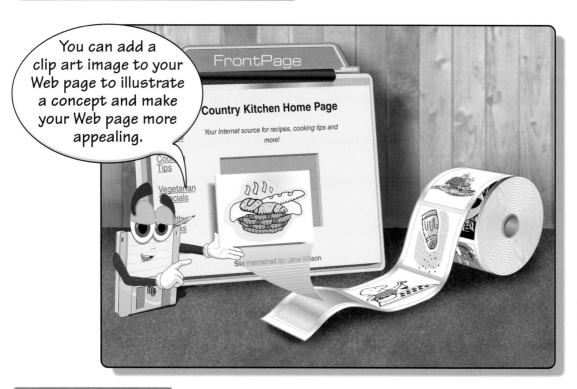

You can add a clip art image to your Web page to illustrate a concept and make your Web page more appealing.

FrontPage organizes clip art images into various categories such as Animals, Business, Entertainment, Nature and Travel.

ADD A CLIP ART IMAGE

1 Click the location on your Web page where you want to add a clip art image.

2 Click **Insert**.

3 Click **Picture**.

4 Click **Clip Art**.

■ The Clip Art Gallery window appears.

■ This area displays the categories of clip art images that FrontPage offers.

5 Click the category of clip art images you want to view.

TIP

Where can I find more clip art images?

If you are connected to the Internet, you can visit Microsoft's Clip Gallery Live Web page to find additional clip art images. In the Clip Art Gallery window, click **Clips Online**. In the dialog box that appears, click **OK** to connect to the Web page. You can also purchase additional clip art images for your Web pages at computer stores.

■ The clip art images in the category you selected appear.

■ To once again view all the categories, click 📖.

6 Click the clip art image you want to add to your Web page. A menu appears.

7 Click 🖼 to add the clip art image to your Web page.

■ The clip art image appears on your Web page.

Note: To move or resize a clip art image, see page 92.

■ To delete a clip art image, click the image and then press the Delete key.

MOVE OR RESIZE AN IMAGE

You can change the location or size of an image on your Web page.

MOVE AN IMAGE

1 Position the mouse I over the image you want to move (I changes to ↘).

2 Drag the image to a new location.

■ The image appears in the new location.

TIP

How can I make an image
appear less distorted?

After you resize an image, you
can use the Resample button (🔳)
to make the image appear less
distorted. To resample an image,
click the image and then click
the Resample button (🔳).

When you resample an image,
the file size of the image will
change. Keep in mind the file
size determines how fast an
image transfers and appears
on a reader's screen.

RESIZE AN IMAGE

1 Click the image you
want to resize. Handles (■)
appear around the image.

2 Position the mouse I
over one of the handles
(I changes to ↘, ↕ or ↔).

3 Drag the image until
the image is the size
you want.

*Note: To keep the image in
proportion, drag a corner handle.*

■ The image appears
in the new size.

*Note: If you make an image
too large, the image may
appear distorted.*

You can add a border to an image on your Web page. This lets you place a frame around the image.

ADD A BORDER TO AN IMAGE

1 Click the image you want to display a border.

2 Click **Format**.

3 Click **Properties**.

■ The Picture Properties dialog box appears.

4 Click the **Appearance** tab.

What color border will appear around an image?

A black border will appear around an image, unless the image is a link. Linked images display a blue border to help people quickly recognize that the image is a link. To create an image link that readers can click to display another Web page, see page 114.

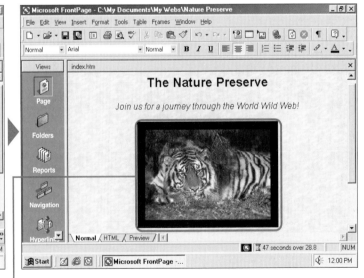

5 Double-click this area and type a thickness for the border in pixels.

Note: A pixel is a dot on a computer screen.

6 Click **OK** to confirm your change.

■ A border appears around the image.

■ To deselect an image, click outside the image.

■ To remove a border from an image, repeat steps **1** to **6**, typing **0** in step **5**.

You can change the way an image appears in relation to the surrounding text.

ALIGN AN IMAGE WITH TEXT

1 Click the image you want to align with text.

Note: The image must appear at the beginning of the text that you want to align with the image. To move an image on your Web page, see page 92.

2 Click **Format**.

3 Click **Properties**.

■ The Picture Properties dialog box appears.

TIP

What are some of the alignment options that FrontPage offers?

Left

Right

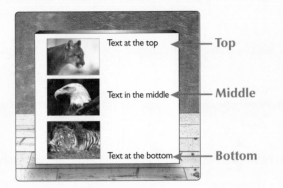

Text at the top — Top

Text in the middle — Middle

Text at the bottom — Bottom

You can use the Left and Right options to wrap a paragraph around an image. The Left option places the image on the left side of the text. The Right option places the image on the right side of the text.

You can use the Top, Middle and Bottom options to vertically align an image with a single line of text.

4 Click the **Appearance** tab.

5 Click this area to display a list of the alignment options.

6 Click the alignment option you want to use.

7 Click **OK** to confirm your selection.

■ The image appears aligned with the text.

ADD A BACKGROUND IMAGE

You can have a small image repeat to fill an entire Web page. This can add an interesting background design to your Web page.

ADD A BACKGROUND IMAGE

1 Click **Format**.

2 Click **Background**.

Note: If Background does not appear on the menu, position the mouse over the bottom of the menu to display all the menu commands.

■ The Page Properties dialog box appears.

3 Click **Background picture** to add a background image to your Web page (☐ changes to ✔).

4 Click **Browse** to locate the image you want to use.

TIP

Where can I find background images?

Many Web sites offer background images you can use for free on your Web pages. You can find a variety of background images, including marble, stone, wood and water. Since background images increase the time Web pages take to appear on a screen, you should choose images with small file sizes that will transfer faster.

You can find background images at the following Web sites:

imagine.metanet.com

www.ip.pt/webground/main.htm

www.nepthys.com/textures

■ The Select Background Picture dialog box appears.

5 Click ![icon] to select the file on your computer that you want to use as the background image.

■ This area displays images you have previously added to your Web site. To use one of these images as your background image, click the image. Press the `Enter` key to select the image and then skip to step **8**.

■ The Select File dialog box appears.

■ This area shows the location of the displayed files. You can click this area to change the location.

6 Click the image you want to use as the background image.

7 Click **OK** to confirm your selection.

CONTINUED

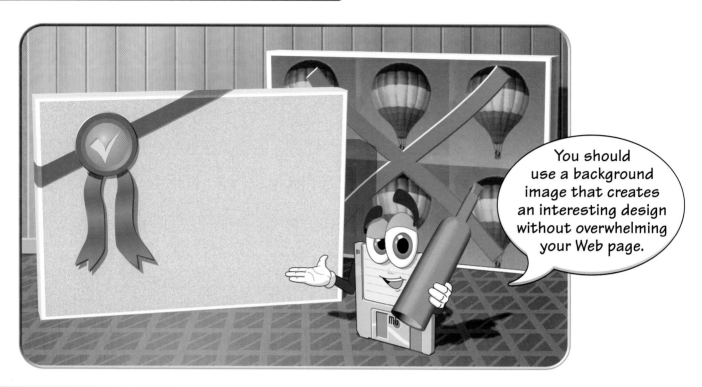

You should use a background image that creates an interesting design without overwhelming your Web page.

ADD A BACKGROUND IMAGE (CONTINUED)

■ This area displays the location and name of the image you selected.

8 Click **OK** to add the background image to your Web page.

■ The image repeats to fill your entire Web page.

TIP

What type of image should I
use as a background image?

Seamless Background

A good background image should
have invisible edges. When the
image repeats to fill the Web page,
you should not be able to tell
where the edges of the images
meet.

Web Page Readability

Make sure the background image
you choose does not affect the
readability of your Web page. You
may need to change the color of text
to make the Web page easier to read.
To change the text color, see page 70.

REMOVE A BACKGROUND IMAGE

1 Click **Format**.

2 Click **Background**.

*Note: If Background does not
appear on the menu, position
the mouse ⌖ over the bottom
of the menu to display all the
menu commands.*

■ The Page Properties
dialog box appears.

3 Click **Background picture**
to remove the background
image from your Web page
(✔ changes to ☐).

4 Click **OK**.

■ The background
image disappears from
your Web page.

CROP AN IMAGE

1 Click the image you want to crop.

2 Click ✂ to crop the image.

Note: If the ✂ button is not displayed, see page 16 to display the Pictures toolbar.

■ A dashed line appears around the image.

3 Position the mouse + over the top left corner of the part of the image you want to keep.

4 Drag the mouse + over the part of the image you want to keep.

Note: If you make a mistake when selecting the area, click outside of the image and then repeat steps 1 to 4.

Why would I crop an image?

You can crop an image to focus a reader's attention on an important part of the image. Cropping an image also lets you change the proportions of an image so the image fits better on your Web page.

When you crop an image, you reduce the file size of the image. This allows the image to transfer more quickly to a reader's screen.

■ A dashed line appears around the area you selected.

5 Click ⌗ to remove all parts of the image outside of the area you selected.

■ All parts of the image outside of the area you selected disappear.

Note: If you previously resized the image, the cropped area will change to the size you specified for the image.

You can create a thumbnail image on your Web page. A thumbnail image is a small version of an image that readers can select to display a larger version of the image.

Thumbnail images allow readers to quickly view the smaller image and decide if they want to wait to view the larger image. Thumbnail images transfer faster and appear on a reader's screen more quickly.

CREATE A THUMBNAIL IMAGE

1 Click the image you want to display as a thumbnail image.

2 Click ![button] to create a thumbnail image.

Note: The Auto Thumbnail button (![button]) is not available if your image is too small to create a thumbnail image or if the image is already a link.

■ A smaller version of the image appears on your Web page.

■ A reader can click the image to view the larger version of the image.

Note: To test the link, you must use the Preview view. For information on the Preview view, see page 40.

■ When you save the Web page, FrontPage will save the new thumbnail image as part of your Web site.

You can make the background of an image transparent so the background will blend into your Web page.

You can make only one color in the background of an image transparent. Every part of the image that displays the color will also become transparent.

You can make only a GIF image transparent. For information on the types of images, see page 86.

MAKE IMAGE BACKGROUND TRANSPARENT

1 Click the image with the background you want to make transparent.

2 Click 🖉.

Note: If 🖉 is not displayed, see page 16 to display the Pictures toolbar.

3 Position the mouse 🖉 over the background of the image and then click to select the background color.

■ The image displays a transparent background.

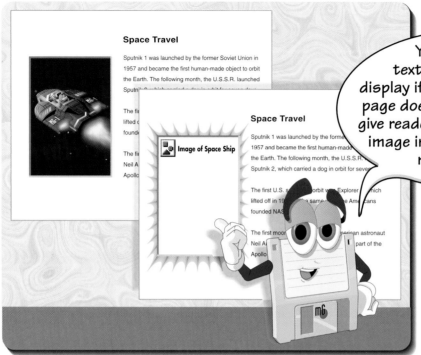

You can provide text that you want to display if an image on your Web page does not appear. This will give readers who do not see the image information about the missing image.

Some readers use Web browsers that cannot display images, while others turn off the display of images to browse the Web more quickly.

PROVIDE ALTERNATIVE TEXT

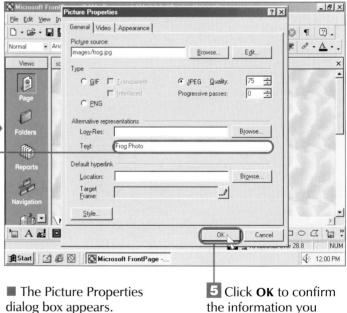

1 Click the image you want to provide alternative text for. Handles (■) appear around the image.

2 Click **Format**.

3 Click **Properties**.

■ The Picture Properties dialog box appears.

4 Click this area and type the text you want to display if the image does not appear.

5 Click **OK** to confirm the information you entered.

You can add a horizontal line to visually separate sections of your Web page.

You should not overuse horizontal lines on your Web page since this can distract your readers and make your Web page difficult to read. Try not to place more than one horizontal line on each screen.

ADD A HORIZONTAL LINE

1 Click the location where you want a horizontal line to appear on your Web page.

2 Click **Insert**.

3 Click **Horizontal Line**.

■ The horizontal line appears on your Web page.

■ To remove a horizontal line, click the line and then press the Delete key.

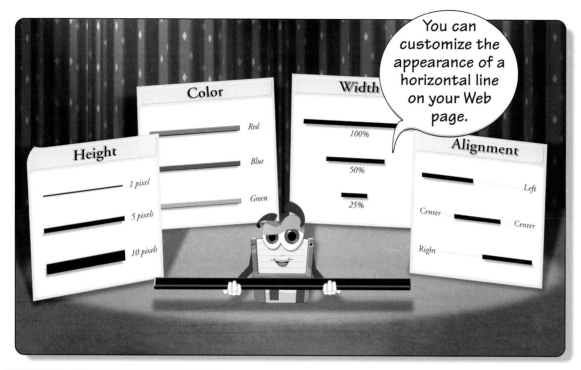

You can customize the appearance of a horizontal line on your Web page.

You can change the height, color, width and alignment of a horizontal line.

If you have applied a theme to your Web page, you cannot customize a horizontal line. To apply a theme, see page 82.

CUSTOMIZE A HORIZONTAL LINE

1 Double-click the horizontal line you want to customize.

■ The Horizontal Line Properties dialog box appears.

2 To change the height of the horizontal line, double-click this area and type a number for the height in pixels.

Note: A pixel is a dot on a computer screen.

3 To change the color of the horizontal line, click this area to display the available colors.

4 Click the color you want to use.

TIP

How can I add a more elaborate horizontal line to my Web page?

You can use an image instead of a horizontal line to visually separate sections of your Web page. You can create your own horizontal line images in an image editing program or obtain images on the Internet.

The following Web sites offer images you can use as horizontal lines:

members.xoom.com/
SSWebGraphics/lines/
lines.htm

www.coolgraphics.com/
gallery.shtml

www.theskull.com/
hor_rule.html

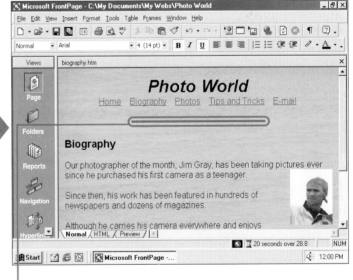

5 To change the percentage of the Web page the horizontal line extends across, double-click this area and type a percentage.

*Note: To extend the horizontal line halfway across your Web page, type **50**.*

6 Click the way you want to align the horizontal line (○ changes to ⊙).

Note: Selecting an alignment will have no effect if the horizontal line width is set at 100.

7 Click **OK**.

■ The appearance of the horizontal line changes.

Note: The Netscape Navigator Web browser will not display a horizontal line in color.

■ To deselect a horizontal line, click outside the horizontal line.

You can create an image map that divides an image into different areas, called hotspots, which each link to a different Web page.

Creating an image map is useful for an image such as a floor plan or map that you want to contain links to different Web pages.

CREATE AN IMAGE MAP

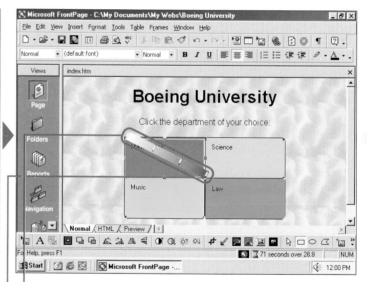

1 Click the image you want to use as an image map. Handles (■) appear around the image. To add an image, see pages 88 to 91.

2 Click the shape you want to use to create a hotspot.

▭ Rectangle

○ Circle

◻ Irregular shape

Note: If the buttons are not displayed, see page 16 to display the Pictures toolbar.

3 Position the mouse I over the area of the image you want to make a hotspot (I changes to ◊).

4 Drag the mouse ◊ until the shape is the size you want.

■ If you selected ◻ in step 2, repeat steps 3 and 4 until you finish drawing all the lines for the shape. Then double-click the mouse to complete the shape.

Note: A hotspot cannot extend beyond the edge of an image.

What should I consider when choosing an image for an image map?

When creating an image map, you should use an image that has several distinct areas that readers can select. Photographs do not usually make good image maps.

 How do I move, resize or delete a hotspot?

You can move or resize a hotspot as you would move or resize any image on your Web page. To move or resize an image, see page 92.

To remove a hotspot, click the hotspot and then press the Delete key.

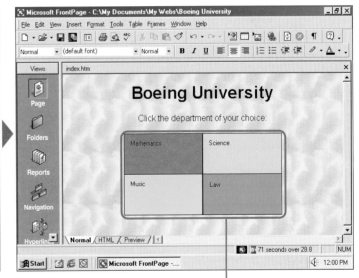

■ The Create Hyperlink dialog box appears.

■ This area displays all the Web pages in your current Web site.

■ 5 To link the hotspot to a Web page in your current Web site, click the Web page.

■ To link the hotspot to a page on the Web, click this area and then type the address of the Web page.

6 Click **OK** to create the link.

■ You can repeat steps 1 to 6 for each hotspot you want to create.

■ To deselect the image and hide the hotspots, click outside the image.

Note: To once again display the hotspots, click the image.

■ A reader can click a hotspot to display the linked Web page.

Note: To test hotspots, you must use the Preview view. For information on the Preview view, see page 40.

Science Today

CHAPTER 7

CREATE LINKS

Would you like to create links that will connect your Web pages to other information on the Internet? Learn how in this chapter.

Chapter 6 - Solar Energy

Solar energy is being used in a variety of ways around the world. For many it is already a way of life. Solar energy is being used to power everything from automobiles to homes.

Great Web Sites
You Can Visit!

1 **Bank of America**
2 **Wal-Mart**
3 **McDonald's**
4 **NBC News**
5 **NFL Football**
6 **Sunkist**
7 **Pepsi**
8 **BMW**

Link

Visited link

Active link

> You can create a link to connect a word, phrase or image on your Web page to another page on the Web.

You can create a link to a Web page in your own Web site or to a Web page created by another person or company.

CREATE A LINK TO ANOTHER WEB PAGE

1 Select the text or click the image you want to link to another Web page. To select text, see page 52.

Note: To add an image, see pages 88 to 91.

2 Click 🖾 to create a link.

■ The Create Hyperlink dialog box appears.

3 To link the text or image to a page on the Web, type the address of the Web page.

■ To link the text or image to a Web page in the current Web site, click the Web page in this area. The area displays all the Web pages in the current Web site.

4 Click **OK** to create the link.

What should I consider when creating a link to another Web page?

Be Descriptive

Make sure the text or image you use for a link clearly indicates where the link will take your readers. Do not use the phrase "Click Here" for a link, since this phrase is not very informative.

Check Your Links

When you create a link to a Web page you did not create, you should verify the link on a regular basis. You may frustrate readers if they select a link that no longer contains relevant information or displays an error message.

■ FrontPage creates the link. Text links appear underlined and in color.

■ To deselect text, click outside the selected area.

■ A reader can click the link to display the Web page you specified.

Note: To test the link, you must use the Preview view. For information on the Preview view, see page 40.

CREATE A LINK AUTOMATICALLY

1 Type the address of a Web page.

2 Press the **Spacebar** or the **Enter** key.

■ FrontPage automatically changes the Web page address to a link.

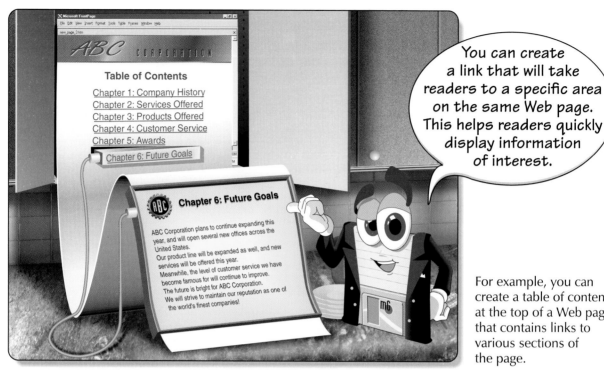

You can create a link that will take readers to a specific area on the same Web page. This helps readers quickly display information of interest.

For example, you can create a table of contents at the top of a Web page that contains links to various sections of the page.

CREATE A LINK WITHIN A WEB PAGE

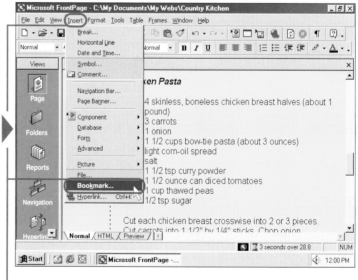

CREATE A BOOKMARK

1 Click the location on the Web page you want readers to be able to quickly display.

2 Click **Insert**.

3 Click **Bookmark**.

Note: If Bookmark does not appear on the menu, position the mouse ⯈ over the bottom of the menu to display all the menu commands.

TIP

What steps are involved for creating a link to a specific area on a Web page?

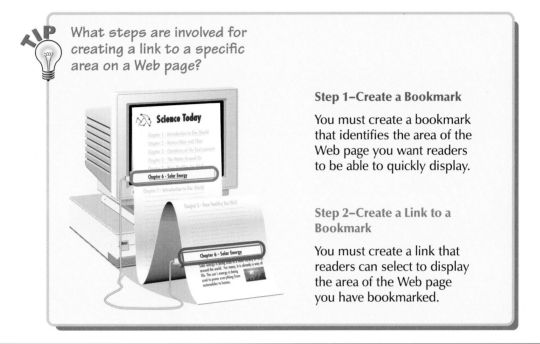

Step 1–Create a Bookmark

You must create a bookmark that identifies the area of the Web page you want readers to be able to quickly display.

Step 2–Create a Link to a Bookmark

You must create a link that readers can select to display the area of the Web page you have bookmarked.

■ The Bookmark dialog box appears.

4 Type a name for the bookmark. Make sure the name clearly describes the Web page area.

5 Click **OK** to save your bookmark.

■ A flag (flag) appears on your Web page. The flag will not appear when you publish your Web page.

■ To delete a bookmark at any time, double-click the flag (flag) and then press the Delete key.

■ You now need to create a link that readers can select to display the area of the Web page you have bookmarked.

CONTINUED

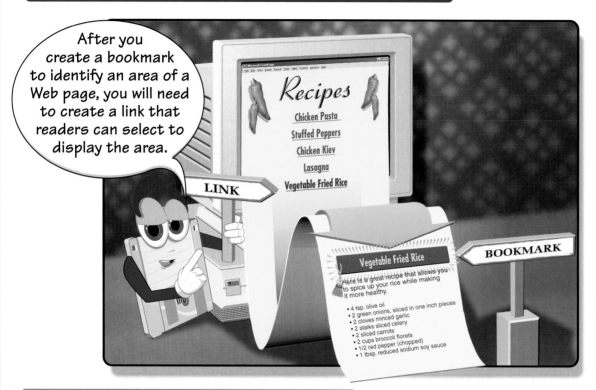

After you create a bookmark to identify an area of a Web page, you will need to create a link that readers can select to display the area.

Make sure the text or image you use for the link clearly indicates where the link will take your readers.

CREATE A LINK WITHIN A WEB PAGE (CONTINUED)

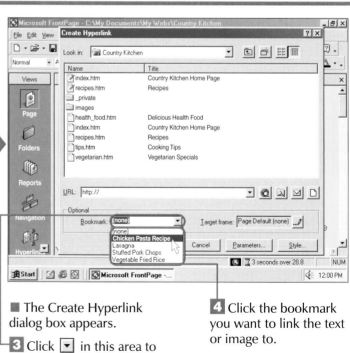

CREATE A LINK TO A BOOKMARK

1 Select the text or click the image you want to link to a bookmark you have created. To select text, see page 52.

Note: To add an image, see pages 88 to 91.

2 Click 🔗 to create a link.

■ The Create Hyperlink dialog box appears.

3 Click ▾ in this area to display a list of bookmarks you have created for the current Web page.

4 Click the bookmark you want to link the text or image to.

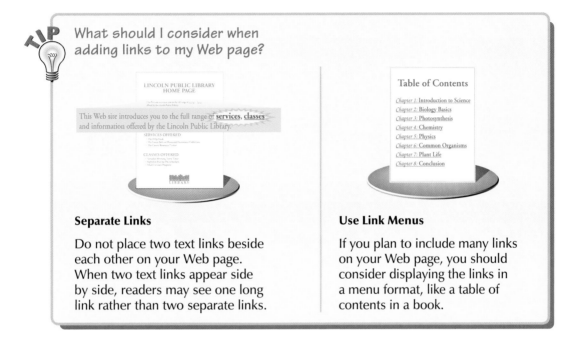

TIP

What should I consider when adding links to my Web page?

Separate Links

Do not place two text links beside each other on your Web page. When two text links appear side by side, readers may see one long link rather than two separate links.

Use Link Menus

If you plan to include many links on your Web page, you should consider displaying the links in a menu format, like a table of contents in a book.

5 Click **OK** to create the link.

■ FrontPage creates the link. Text links appear underlined and in color.

■ To deselect text, click outside the selected area.

■ A reader can click the link to display the Web page area you specified.

Note: To test the link, you must use the Preview view. For information on the Preview view, see page 40.

You can create a link on your Web page that allows readers to quickly send you an e-mail message.

When a reader selects an e-mail link, a blank message addressed to you will appear.

CREATE AN E-MAIL LINK

1 Select the text or click the image you want readers to select to send you an e-mail message. To select text, see page 52.

Note: To add an image, see pages 88 to 91.

2 Click 🖼 to create a link.

■ The Create Hyperlink dialog box appears.

3 Click ✉ to create an e-mail link.

Why should I include an e-mail link on my Web page?

An e-mail link allows readers to send you questions and comments that can help you improve your Web pages. Many companies include a list of e-mail links that allow you to contact employees in different departments.

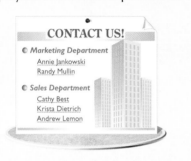

Why should I include an e-mail link on my Web page?

Can FrontPage automatically create an e-mail link?

When you type an e-mail address on your Web page, FrontPage will automatically change the address to a link for you.

jsmith@abc.com

■ The Create E-mail Hyperlink dialog box appears.

4 Type the e-mail address of the person you want to receive the messages. In most cases, you will enter your own e-mail address.

5 Click **OK** to confirm the information you entered.

6 Click **OK** to create the e-mail link.

■ FrontPage creates the e-mail link. Text e-mail links appear underlined and in color.

■ To deselect text, click outside the selected area.

■ A reader can click the e-mail link to send a message to the e-mail address you specified.

Note: To test the link, you must use the Preview view. For information on the Preview view, see page 40.

You can create a link on your Web page that readers can select to play a sound.

You can provide entertaining sound clips from television shows, movies and famous speeches. You can also add sound clips to provide samples of your products, such as music CDs or audiotapes.

The most common types of sounds on the Web are MIDI, MPEG, RealAudio and Wave.

CREATE A LINK TO A SOUND

■ Before you can create a link to a sound on your Web page, you must add the sound file to the folder that stores all the Web pages for your Web site. For more information, see the top of page 123.

■ The sound file you add to the folder will appear in the Folder List.

Note: If the sound file does not appear in the Folder List, click the Folder List area and then press the F5 key to refresh the list.

1 Select the text or click the image you want readers to select to play the sound. To select text, see page 52.

Note: To add an image, see pages 88 to 91.

2 Click 🖲 to create a link.

What do I need to do before I can create a link to a sound on my Web page?

You need to place a copy of the sound file in the same folder that stores all the Web pages for your Web site. This ensures the sound file will transfer with your Web site when you publish your Web pages. If you do not copy the sound file, people will not be able to play the sound.

Each Web site you create has its own folder in the My Webs folder. The My Webs folder is stored in the My Documents folder on your C drive.

Where can I obtain sounds?

You can purchase collections of sounds at computer stores and also obtain sounds on the Internet. You can find sounds at the following Web sites.

earthstation1.com   wavcentral.com

soundamerica.com

■ The Create Hyperlink dialog box appears.

■ This area displays the files in the current Web site.

3 Click the sound file you want to link to the text or image.

4 Click **OK** to create the link.

■ FrontPage creates the link. Text links appear underlined and in color.

■ To deselect text, click outside the selected area.

■ When a reader selects the sound link, the sound will transfer to their computer and play.

Note: To test the link, you must use the Preview view. For information on the Preview view, see page 40.

You can create a link on your Web page that readers can select to play a video.

You can provide entertaining videos such as visual effects, movie clips, animation and home videos. You can also add videos to provide information about your company, organization or topic of interest.

The most common types of videos on the Web are AVI, MPEG, QuickTime and RealVideo.

CREATE A LINK TO A VIDEO

■ Before you can create a link to a video on your Web page, you must add the video file to the folder that stores all the Web pages for your Web site. For more information, see the top of page 125.

■ The video file you add to the folder will appear in the Folder List.

Note: If the video file does not appear in the Folder List, click the Folder List area and then press the **F5** *key to refresh the list.*

1 Select the text or click the image you want readers to select to play the video. To select text, see page 52.

Note: To add an image, see pages 88 to 91.

2 Click 🔖 to create a link.

124

What do I need to do before I can create a link to a video on my Web page?

You need to place a copy of the video file in the same folder that stores all the Web pages for your Web site. This ensures the video file will transfer with your Web site when you publish your Web pages. If you do not copy the video file, people will not be able to play the video.

Each Web site you create has its own folder in the My Webs folder. The My Webs folder is stored in the My Documents folder on your C drive.

Where can I obtain videos?

You can purchase collections of videos at computer stores and also obtain videos on the Internet. You can find videos at the following Web sites.

www.jurassicpunk.com

www.nasa.gov/gallery/video

■ The Create Hyperlink dialog box appears.

■ This area displays the files in the current Web site.

3 Click the video file you want to link to the text or image.

4 Click **OK** to create the link.

■ FrontPage creates the link. Text links appear underlined and in color.

■ To deselect text, click outside the selected area.

■ When a reader selects the video link, the video will transfer to their computer and play.

Note: To test the link, you must use the Preview view. For information on the Preview view, see page 40.

125

You can change the color of links on your Web page.

A Web page can contain three types of links.

Link
A link a reader has not previously selected.

Visited link
A link a reader has previously selected.

Active link
A link a reader is currently selecting.

CHANGE LINK COLORS

1 Click **Format**.

2 Click **Background**.

Note: If Background does not appear on the menu, position the mouse ⟍ over the bottom of the menu to display all the menu commands.

■ The Page Properties dialog box appears.

■ This area displays the colors currently used for links, visited links and active links.

TIP

What should I consider when
changing the color of links?

Change Only When Necessary

You may confuse some readers if you
do not use the standard link colors.
You should change link colors only
when necessary, such as when the
background color you are using
makes the links difficult to read.

Choose Different Colors

Make sure you choose different colors
for links, visited links and active links
so you can clearly distinguish between
the types of links. By default, links
are blue, visited links are purple and
active links are red.

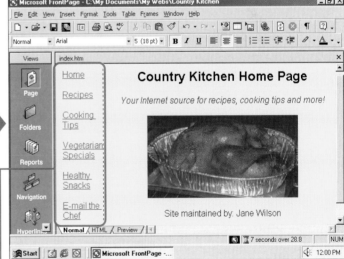

3 Click the area beside
the type of link you want
to display in a different
color.

4 Click the color you
want to use.

5 To change the color
for another type of link,
repeat steps 3 and 4 for
each link.

6 Click **OK** to confirm
your changes.

■ The links on your Web
page appear in the colors
you selected.

■ To return a link to its
original color, repeat
steps 1 to 6, selecting
Automatic in step 4.

*Note: To test a link, you must
use the Preview view. For
information on the Preview
view, see page 40.*

You can remove a link from text or an image on your Web page.

Removing a link will not remove the text or image for the link from your Web page.

1 Click the text or image for the link you want to remove.

2 Click 🖫 to display the information for the link.

■ The Edit Hyperlink dialog box appears.

3 To select the information in this area, drag the mouse I over the text until you highlight all the information.

4 Press the Delete key to delete the information.

7

TIP

How do I remove a link as well as the text or image for the link?

To remove a link as well as the text or image for the link, select the text or click the image and then press the Delete key.

You may want to remove a link that takes readers to a Web page that no longer contains relevant information. Many companies and individuals regularly make changes to their Web pages, so you should check your links often and remove links that are no longer useful.

■ The information disappears.

5 Click **OK** to confirm your change.

■ FrontPage removes the link from the text or image.

■ Text links no longer appear underlined and in color. The appearance of image links does not change.

■ To deselect text, click outside the selected area.

You can use the Hyperlinks view to display the links that connect each Web page to other pages in your Web site.

The Hyperlinks view helps you review the links you have added to your Web pages. This can help you determine if you forgot to add links to a Web page.

USING THE HYPERLINKS VIEW

1 Click Hyperlinks to display your Web site in the Hyperlinks view.

■ This area displays a list of all the Web pages (📄) in your Web site.

■ If the list does not appear, click 📰 to display the list.

2 Click the Web page that contains the links you want to display.

■ An icon for the Web page you selected appears in this area. The file name of the Web page appears below the icon.

■ FrontPage displays the links to and from the Web page.

TIP

What does each icon represent in the Hyperlinks view?

	A link to a Web page within your Web site.
	A link to a Web page on the Web.
	A link to an e-mail address.

TIP

Why do links I didn't create appear in my Web site?

When you use a template or wizard to create your Web site, FrontPage may add links to the Web pages for you. To create a Web site using a template or wizard, see page 28.

■ If the icon for a Web page displays a plus sign (⊞), the Web page contains links to other pages.

3 To display the Web pages that link to the page, click the plus sign (⊞).

■ The Web pages linked to the page appear.

■ You may need to use the scroll bar to view the linked Web pages.

■ You can click the minus sign (⊟) to once again hide the linked Web pages (⊟ changes to ⊞).

You can check the links in your Web site to determine if the links are working correctly.

You must be connected to the Internet to check links to Web pages you did not create.

Before checking the links in your Web site, make sure you save all your Web pages. This ensures that you check the most current versions of the pages.

CHECK LINKS

1 Click **Reports** to display your Web site in the Reports view.

2 Click 🖳 to check the links in your Web site.

Note: If the Reporting toolbar is not displayed, see page 16 to display the toolbar.

■ The Verify Hyperlinks dialog box appears.

3 Click **Verify all hyperlinks** to check all the links in your Web site (○ changes to ⊙).

4 Click **Start** to begin checking the links.

TIP

Why is a link in my Web site broken?

A link that has an incorrect Web page address is called a broken link. When a reader clicks a broken link, an error message will appear. A link may not work for the following reasons:

▶ You typed the Web page address incorrectly.

▶ You deleted the Web page the link connects to.

▶ The Web page was moved or deleted on the Web.

Should I check the links on my Web pages manually?

You should manually check the links that connect to Web pages you did not create. Companies and individuals often change the content of their Web pages and the content may no longer relate to your pages.

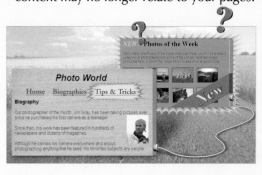

■ FrontPage displays the Broken Hyperlinks report, which displays each link in your Web site.

■ As FrontPage checks the links, this area displays the status of each link (✓ OK, 🔗 Broken).

REPAIR A BROKEN LINK

You can repair any broken links in your Web site.

1 Double-click a broken link that you want to repair.

■ The Edit Hyperlink dialog box appears.

2 Type the correct Web page address for the link. Make sure you start the address with **http://**.

■ This area displays all the pages in your Web site that contain the link.

3 Click **Replace** to replace every occurrence of the link on your Web pages.

133

CHAPTER 8

CREATE TABLES

Do you want to use tables to help you organize information on your Web pages? Find out how in this chapter.

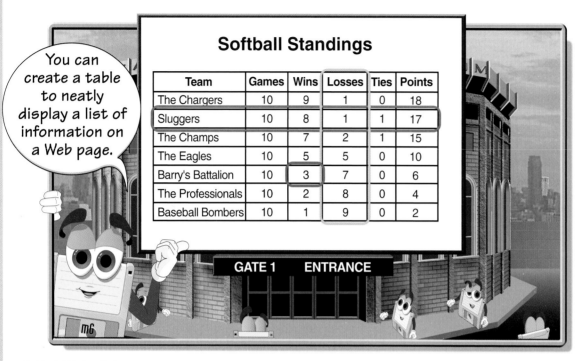

You can create a table to neatly display a list of information on a Web page.

Softball Standings

Team	Games	Wins	Losses	Ties	Points
The Chargers	10	9	1	0	18
Sluggers	10	8	1	1	17
The Champs	10	7	2	1	15
The Eagles	10	5	5	0	10
Barry's Battalion	10	3	7	0	6
The Professionals	10	2	8	0	4
Baseball Bombers	10	1	9	0	2

GATE 1   ENTRANCE

A table consists of rows, columns and cells.

A **row** is a horizontal line of boxes.

A **column** is a vertical line of boxes.

A **cell** is one box.

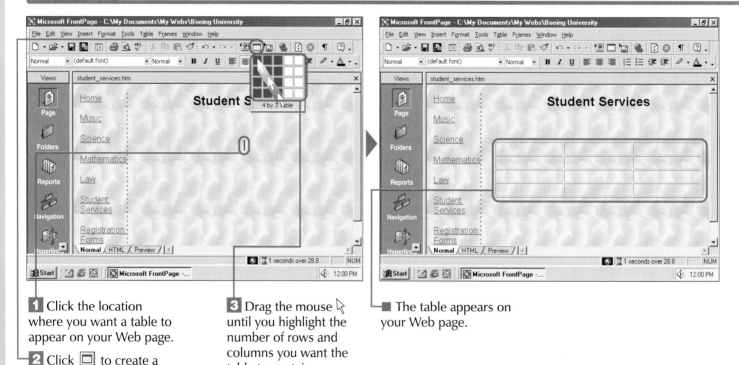

1 Click the location where you want a table to appear on your Web page.

2 Click 🔲 to create a table.

3 Drag the mouse until you highlight the number of rows and columns you want the table to contain.

■ The table appears on your Web page.

What other ways can I use a table on a Web page?

Create Newspaper Columns

You can use tables to present information in columns like those found in a newspaper. To display information in three newspaper columns, you can create a table with one row that contains three cells.

Control Web Page Layout

Tables are useful for controlling the placement of text and images on a Web page. To neatly position two paragraphs and two images, you can create a table with two rows and two columns.

DELETE A TABLE

ENTER TEXT IN A TABLE

1 Click the cell where you want to enter text. Then type the text.

2 Repeat step **1** until you finish entering all the text.

1 Position the mouse I to the left of the table you want to delete (I changes to ⇗). Then double-click to select the table.

2 Click ✂ to delete the table.

You can add a row or column to your table to insert additional information.

ADD A ROW OR COLUMN

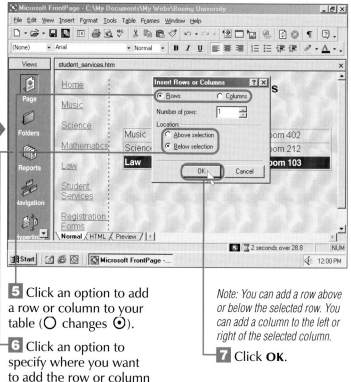

1 Position the mouse I to the left of the row or above the column where you want to add a new row or column (I changes to → or ↓). Then click to select the row or column.

2 Click **Table**.

3 Click **Insert**.

4 Click **Rows or Columns**.

■ The Insert Rows or Columns dialog box appears.

5 Click an option to add a row or column to your table (○ changes ◉).

6 Click an option to specify where you want to add the row or column (○ changes to ◉).

Note: You can add a row above or below the selected row. You can add a column to the left or right of the selected column.

7 Click **OK**.

138

How can I quickly add a row to the bottom of a table?

To quickly add a row to the bottom of a table, click the bottom right cell in the table. Then press the Tab key.

Can I delete the information in a row or column without removing the row or column from a table?

Yes. To select the cells that contain the information you want to delete, drag the mouse I over the cells. Then press the Delete key to remove the information.

■ The new row or column appears in your table.

■ To deselect a row or column, click outside the table.

DELETE A ROW OR COLUMN

1 Position the mouse I to the left of the row or above the column you want to delete (I changes to ➜ or ↓). Then click to select the row or column.

2 Click ✂ to delete the row or column you selected.

You can change the height of rows and the width of columns to improve the layout of a table.

CHANGE ROW HEIGHT

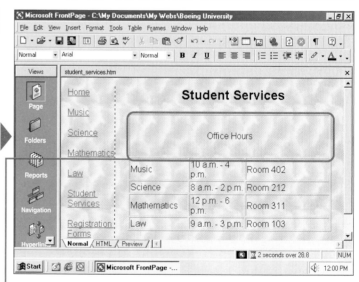

1 Position the mouse I over the bottom edge of the row you want to change (I changes to ↕).

2 Drag the row edge to a new position.

■ A dotted line shows the new position.

■ The row displays the new height.

TIP

Will FrontPage ever automatically adjust the row height or column width?

When you enter text in a table, FrontPage automatically increases the row height or column width to accommodate the text you type.

TIP

Can I make the row height or column width any size?

You can make the row height or column width any size you want. However, FrontPage will not allow you to make the row or column too small to display the text or image in a cell.

CHANGE COLUMN WIDTH

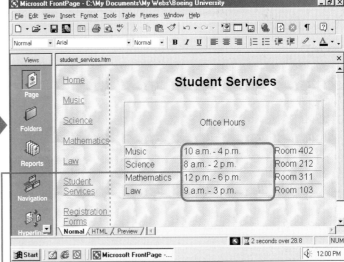

1 Position the mouse I over the right edge of the column you want to change (I changes to ↔).

2 Drag the column edge to a new position.

■ A dotted line shows the new position.

■ The column displays the new width.

Note: When you change the column width for the last column, the width of the entire table changes.

You can combine two or more cells in a table to make one large cell. This is useful if you want to display a title across the top or down the side of a table.

Pool A

Team	Games	Wins	Losses	Ties	Points
The Cha...ers	10	9	1	0	18
Slugg...s	10	8	1	1	17
...namps	10	7	2	1	15
...e Eagles	10	5	5	0	10

COMBINE CELLS

1 Position the mouse I over the first cell you want to merge with other cells.

2 Drag the mouse I until you highlight all the cells you want to merge.

3 Click **Table**.

4 Click **Merge Cells**.

■ The cells combine to create one large cell.

■ To deselect cells in a table, click outside the table.

142

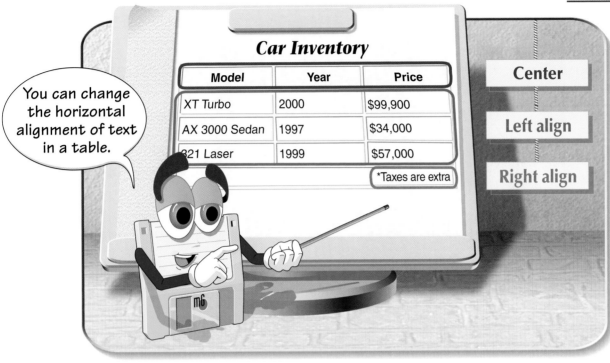

You can change the horizontal alignment of text in a table.

Center

Left align

Right align

CHANGE ALIGNMENT OF TEXT

1 Position the mouse I over the first cell that contains the text you want to align differently.

2 Drag the mouse I until you highlight all the cells that contain the text you want to align differently.

3 Click one of the following options.

▤ Left align

▤ Center

▤ Right align

■ The text appears in the new alignment.

■ To deselect cells in a table, click outside the table.

You can add an image to a cell in your table. Tables allow you to control the placement of images and text on your Web page.

To obtain images that you can add to a table, see page 87.

1 Click the cell in the table where you want to add an image.

2 Click 🖼 to add an image.

■ The Picture dialog box appears.

3 Click 🔍 to locate the image on your computer that you want to use.

■ This area displays images you have previously added to your Web site. To add one of these images, click the image. Then press the Enter key to add the image.

TIP

How do tables control the placement of images and text on a Web page?

Tables provide a structure for images and text on a Web page. For example, to neatly position two paragraphs and two images, you can create a table with two rows and two columns.

When you use a table to organize information on a Web page, you may want to remove the border to make the table invisible. To remove the border from a table, see the top of page 149.

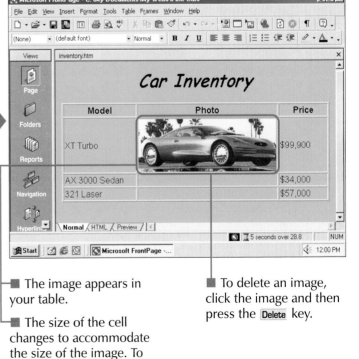

■ The Select File dialog box appears.

■ This area shows the location of the displayed files. You can click this area to change the location.

4 Click the image you want to add to your table.

5 Click **OK** to confirm your selection.

■ The image appears in your table.

■ The size of the cell changes to accommodate the size of the image. To resize an image, see page 93.

■ To delete an image, click the image and then press the Delete key.

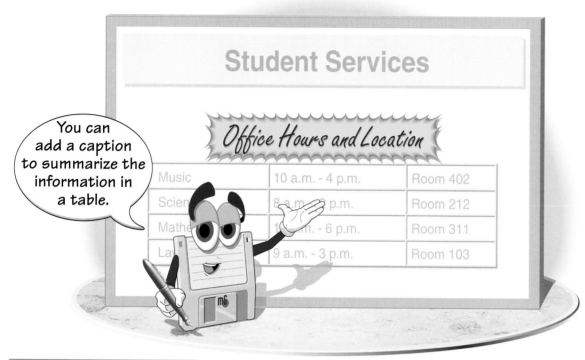

You can add a caption to summarize the information in a table.

Captions are automatically centered at the top of a table.

ADD A CAPTION TO A TABLE

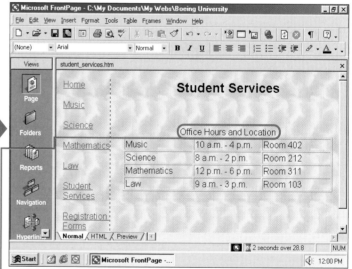

1 Click anywhere inside the table you want to display a caption.

2 Click **Table**.

3 Click **Insert**.

4 Click **Caption**.

■ A flashing insertion point appears above the table.

5 Type the caption you want the table to display.

■ To delete a caption, click to the left of the caption to select the caption. Then press the **Delete** key.

You can add a background color to cells in a table to enhance the appearance of the table.

To change the color of text in a table, see page 70.

ADD COLOR TO CELLS

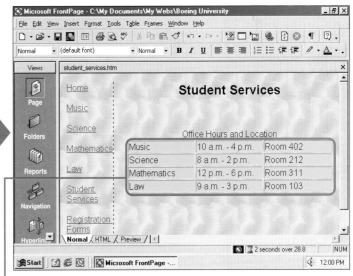

1 Position the mouse I over the first cell in the table you want to add color to.

2 Drag the mouse I until you highlight all the cells you want to add color to.

3 Click ▾ in this area to display the available colors.

4 Click the color you want to use.

■ The cells in the table display the color you selected.

■ To deselect cells in a table, click outside the table.

■ To remove color from cells in a table, repeat steps **1** to **4**, selecting **Automatic** in step **4**.

You can change the size of the border that surrounds a table. You can also change the color of the border.

CHANGE TABLE BORDER

1 Click anywhere in the table that displays the border you want to change.

2 Click **Table**.

3 Click **Properties**.

4 Click **Table**.

■ The Table Properties dialog box appears.

5 Double-click this area and type the size you want to use for the border.

TIP

How do I specify the size of a border around a table?

You specify the size of a border around a table in pixels. A pixel is a dot on a computer screen. The word "pixel" comes from **pic**ture **el**ement.

1 Pixel

2 Pixels

3 Pixels

4 Pixels

5 Pixels

TIP

Can I remove a border from a table?

Yes. When you are using a table to organize the information on a Web page, you can remove the border to make the table invisible. To remove the border from a table, use a border size of **0**.

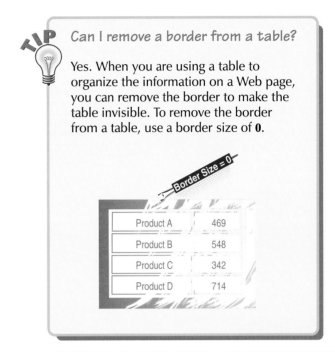

Border Size = 0

Product A	469
Product B	548
Product C	342
Product D	714

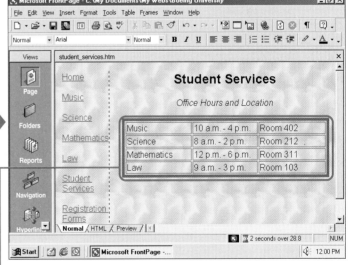

-6 To select a color for the border, click this area to display the available colors.

-7 Click the color you want to use for the border.

-8 Click **OK** to confirm your changes.

■ The table displays the border size and color you selected.

■ To return to the original border color, repeat steps 1 to 8, selecting **Automatic** in step 7.

NAVIGATION VIEW

Home Page

Services

Music

Mathematics

Science

School Band

Science Fair

Navigation Buttons
to Appear on Web Pages

CHAPTER 9

WORK WITH NAVIGATIONAL STRUCTURE

Are you wondering how to arrange the Web pages in your Web site? This chapter shows how to build the structure of your Web site.

You can use the Navigation view to work with the navigational structure of your Web site.

The Navigation view shows how the pages in your Web site are related.

USING THE NAVIGATION VIEW

1 Click **Navigation** to display your Web site in the Navigation view.

■ This area displays all the Web pages (▣) in your Web site.

■ If the list does not appear, click ▣ to display the list.

■ This area displays the navigational structure of your Web site.

■ Each box represents one Web page. The title of the Web page appears in the box.

■ Lines between the boxes indicate how the Web pages are related.

Note: FrontPage may automatically set up the navigational structure for the Web site when you create the Web site. If the area appears blank, you need to add Web pages to the navigational structure. To add Web pages, see page 154.

TIP

Why should I work with the navigational structure of my Web site?

The navigational structure of your Web site determines which navigation buttons appear on your Web pages. Navigation buttons are links readers can select to move through the pages in your Web site. When you change the navigational structure of your Web site, FrontPage automatically updates the navigation buttons for you. To change the navigational structure of your Web site, see pages 154 to 156. To add navigation buttons to your Web pages, see page 158.

■ If the box for a Web page displays a minus sign (⊟), one or more pages appear below the page.

Note: Hiding Web pages allows you to hide pages that are currently not of interest so you can focus on other pages.

2 To hide the Web pages below a page, click the minus sign (⊟).

■ The Web pages are hidden from view.

■ You can click the plus sign (⊞) to once again display the Web pages below the page (⊞ changes to ⊟).

You can add Web pages in the Navigation view to build the navigational structure of your Web site.

When you add navigation buttons to your Web pages, any Web pages you add to the navigational structure will appear as navigation buttons on your Web pages. To add navigation buttons to your Web pages, see page 158.

ADD A WEB PAGE TO THE WEB SITE STRUCTURE

1 Click **Navigation** to display your Web site in the Navigation view.

2 Position the mouse over the Web page you want to add to the navigational structure of your Web site.

3 Drag the mouse to where you want to add the Web page.

Note: A gray outline shows where the Web page will appear.

■ The Web page appears in the navigational structure of your Web site.

■ You can repeat steps 2 and 3 for each Web page you want to add.

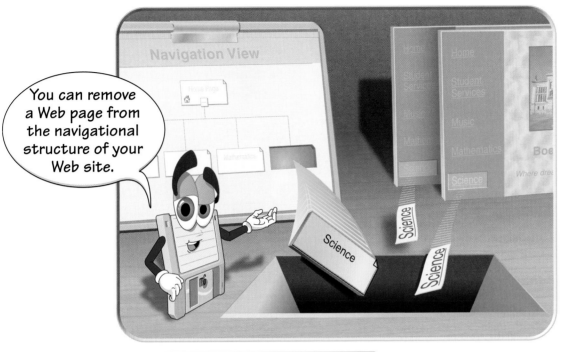

You can remove a Web page from the navigational structure of your Web site.

When you add navigation buttons to your Web pages, any Web pages you remove from the navigational structure will no longer appear as navigation buttons on your Web pages. To add navigation buttons to your Web pages, see page 158.

REMOVE A WEB PAGE FROM THE WEB SITE STRUCTURE

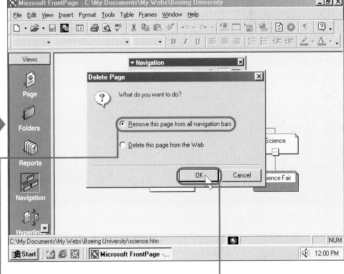

1 Click **Navigation** to display your Web site in the Navigation view.

2 Click the Web page you want to remove from the navigational structure of your Web site.

3 Press the `Delete` key to remove the Web page.

■ The Delete Page dialog box appears.

4 Click this option to delete the Web page from the navigational structure of your Web site (○ changes to ⊙).

5 Click **OK**.

Note: When you delete a Web page from the navigational structure of your Web site, you do not delete the page from your Web site.

MOVE A WEB PAGE IN THE WEB SITE STRUCTURE

You can rearrange Web pages to better organize the information in your Web site.

When you add navigation buttons to your Web pages, rearranging Web pages in the navigational structure will change which navigation buttons appear on your Web pages and the order of the navigation buttons. To add navigation buttons to your Web pages, see page 158.

MOVE A WEB PAGE IN THE WEB SITE STRUCTURE

1 Click **Navigation** to display your Web site in the Navigation view.

2 Position the mouse over the Web page you want to move.

3 Drag the Web page to where you want the page to appear in your Web site structure.

Note: A gray outline shows where the Web page will appear.

■ The Web page appears in the new location.

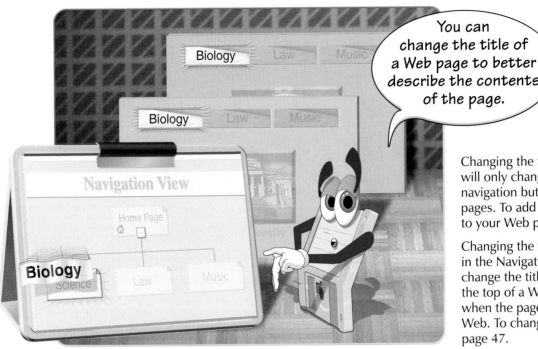

> You can change the title of a Web page to better describe the contents of the page.

Changing the titles of Web pages will only change the labels for navigation buttons on your Web pages. To add navigation buttons to your Web pages, see page 158.

Changing the title of a Web page in the Navigation view will not change the title that appears at the top of a Web browser window when the page appears on the Web. To change this title, see page 47.

CHANGE WEB PAGE TITLE IN THE WEB SITE STRUCTURE

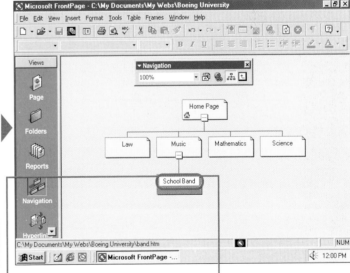

1 Click **Navigation** to display your Web site in the Navigation view.

2 Click the title of the Web page you want to change.

3 Wait a moment and then click the title of the Web page again.

■ The title of the Web page appears in a box.

4 Type a new title for the Web page and then press the **Enter** key.

You can add shared borders to every page in your Web site. Shared borders allow you to display the same information on every Web page.

Shared borders can display navigation buttons that are links readers can select to move through the pages in your Web site. You can also add information to shared borders such as images, contact numbers, copyright information or a company logo.

ADD SHARED BORDERS

1 Click **Format**.

2 Click **Shared Borders**.

Note: If Shared Borders does not appear on the menu, position the mouse ▨ over the bottom of the menu to display all the menu commands.

■ The Shared Borders dialog box appears.

3 Click **All pages** to add a shared border to every Web page in your Web site (○ changes to ◉).

4 Click an option to specify where you want the shared border to appear on every Web page (☐ changes to ☑).

■ A dashed line indicates where the shared border will appear on your Web pages.

How does FrontPage determine which navigation buttons to place on my Web pages?

FrontPage sets up navigation buttons based on the structure of your Web site in the Navigation view. To use the Navigation view, see pages 152 to 157.

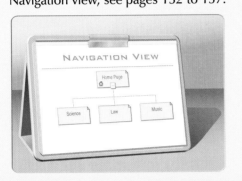

What labels will FrontPage use for navigation buttons?

The titles of your Web pages determine the labels for navigation buttons. To change the title of a Web page, see page 157.

5 If you selected **Top** or **Left** in step 4, click **Include navigation buttons** to display navigation buttons on your Web pages (☐ changes to ☑).

Note: Only the top and left shared borders allow you to display navigation buttons.

6 Click **OK** to save your changes.

■ All the Web pages in your Web site display the shared border.

■ If you chose to include navigation buttons in step 5, the buttons will appear in the shared border.

■ You need to apply a theme to your Web page to display graphical navigation buttons. To apply a theme, see page 82.

■ To remove a shared border from all the pages in your Web site, repeat steps 1 to 4 (☑ changes to ☐ in step 4). Then perform step 6.

Once you add navigation buttons to your Web pages, you can specify which navigation buttons you want to appear on the pages. You can also change the orientation and appearance of the navigation buttons.

Navigation buttons are links readers can select to move through the pages in your Web site. To add navigation buttons to your Web pages, see page 158.

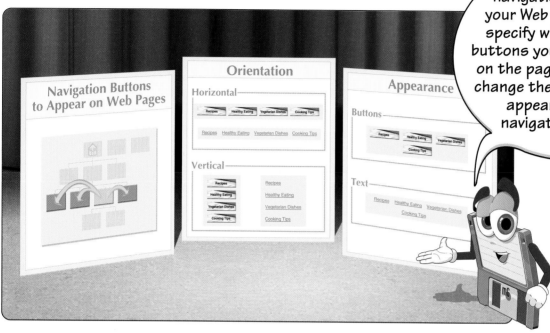

CHANGE NAVIGATION BUTTONS IN SHARED BORDERS

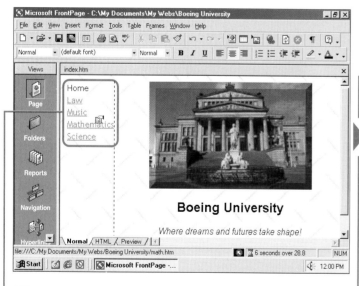

1 Double-click a navigation button on a Web page.

Note: If your Web page does not display navigation buttons, double-click the text that appears in the navigation button area.

■ The Navigation Bar Properties dialog box appears.

2 Click an option to specify which links you want to appear on your Web pages (○ changes to ⊙).

■ This area shows the links that will appear on your Web pages.

■ These options add links to the home page and the page above the current page. If you do not want to display these links, click an option to turn the option off (☑ changes to ☐).

TIP What navigation buttons can I add to my Web pages?

Parent level
Include links to pages directly above the current page.

Same level
Include links to pages on the same level as the current page.

Back and next
Include links to pages beside the current page.

Child level
Include links to pages directly below the current page.

Top level
Include links to pages on the same level as the home page.

Child pages under Home
Include links to pages directly below the home page.

3 Click an option to display the links side by side (Horizontal) or in a list (Vertical) (○ changes to ⊙).

4 Click an option to display the links as graphical buttons or as text (○ changes to ⊙).

5 Click **OK** to confirm your changes.

■ The navigation buttons display the changes.

■ If you selected **Buttons** in step 4, you need to apply a theme to your Web page to display graphical navigation buttons. To apply a theme, see page 82.

CHAPTER 10

CREATE FRAMES

Would you like to display your Web pages in frames? This chapter shows you how to create and work with frames.

You can create frames to divide a Web browser window into sections. Each section will display a different Web page.

To create frames, you must create a frames page. A frames page provides the structure for displaying several Web pages at the same time.

FrontPage offers several ready-to-use templates that you can choose from to quickly create frames.

CREATE FRAMES

1 Click **File**.

2 Click **New**.

3 Click **Page**.

■ The New dialog box appears.

4 Click the **Frames Pages** tab.

■ This area displays the frames templates that FrontPage offers.

5 Click the frames template you want to use.

Why would I use frames?

Frames allow you to display information on a Web page that will remain on the screen while readers browse through your Web pages.

Banners

Frames can display information such as an advertisement, a warning message or a company logo.

Navigation

Frames can display a table of contents or navigational tools to help readers move through your Web pages and find information of interest.

Supporting Information

Frames can display supporting information such as copyright notices or footnotes.

■ A description of the frames template you selected appears in this area.

■ A preview of the frames template appears in this area.

6 Click **OK** to create the frames.

■ A blank frames page based on the template you selected appears.

■ You can now specify which Web page you want to appear in each frame. To add a Web page to a frame, see pages 166 to 168.

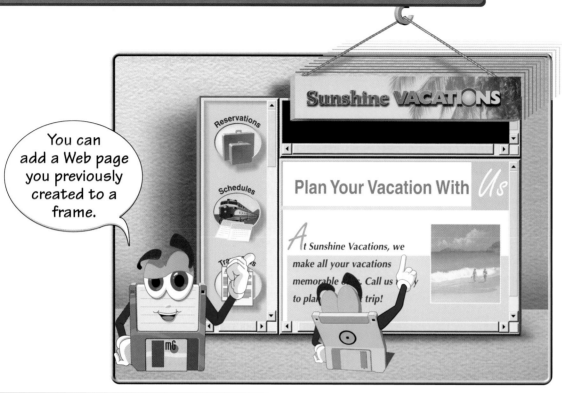

You can add a Web page you previously created to a frame.

1 Click **Set Initial Page** to add a Web page you previously created to a frame.

Note: If the Set Initial Page button is not displayed, see page 164 to create frames.

■ The Create Hyperlink dialog box appears.

■ This area displays all the Web pages in your current Web site.

2 Click the Web page you want to appear in the frame.

What should I consider when adding Web pages to frames?

You should check how the Web pages displayed in your frames appear on computers with monitors using different resolutions. The resolution of a monitor determines the amount of information that will appear in each frame. Monitors using lower resolutions will show less information in each frame. For example, a heading or image may not fully appear in a frame on monitors using lower resolutions.

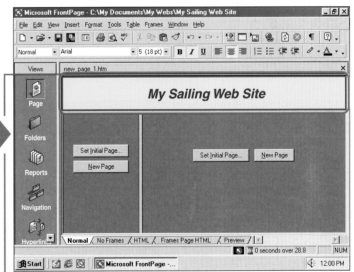

3 Click **OK** to add the Web page to the frame.

■ The Web page appears in the frame.

■ You can repeat steps **1** to **3** for each frame you want to display a Web page you previously created.

Once you create frames, you can add a new Web page to a frame.

ADD A NEW WEB PAGE TO A FRAME

1 Click **New Page** to add a new Web page to a frame.

Note: If the New Page button is not displayed, see page 164 to create frames.

■ A new Web page appears in the frame.

■ You can immediately add information to the Web page.

> You can easily change the size of a frame.

Resizing a frame will not affect the information displayed in the frame. Resizing a frame only changes how much information the frame displays.

RESIZE A FRAME

1 Position the mouse I over the border of the frame you want to resize (I changes to ↕ or ↔).

2 Drag the mouse ↕ until the frame is the size you want.

■ The frame displays the new size.

■ The new frame size affects the size of adjacent frames.

You should save your frames to store the frames for future use. This lets you later review and edit the Web pages displayed in the frames.

When you save frames, FrontPage will ask you to save each new Web page you added to a frame and the frames page. The frames page provides the structure for displaying several Web pages at the same time.

SAVE FRAMES

1 Click 🖫 to save your frames.

■ The Save As dialog box appears.

■ This area displays the layout of the frames. If you added a new Web page to a frame, the frame appears highlighted.

Note: If you did not add a new Web page to a frame, skip to step 5.

■ This area shows the location where FrontPage will store the new Web page.

Note: FrontPage will automatically store your Web page in the folder for the current Web site.

Why does the Save Embedded Files dialog box appear when I save my frames?

If you added an image to a Web page displayed in a frame, you need to save the image as part of your Web site. A copy of the image will be stored in the same folder that stores all the Web pages for your Web site. This ensures the image will transfer with your Web site when you publish your Web pages.

1 Click **OK** to save the image.

2 Type a file name for the Web page.

*Note: A Web page file name should not include spaces or unusual characters, such as * or #.*

3 Click **Save** to save the Web page.

4 You will need to repeat steps 2 and 3 for each new Web page you added to a frame.

■ When you finish saving each new Web page you added to your frames, FrontPage allows you to save the frames page, which provides the structure for displaying the frames.

■ When saving the frames page, a heavy border appears around the frames in this area.

5 Type a file name for the frames page.

6 Click **Save** to save the frames page.

You can create a link on a Web page that readers can select to display a Web page in another frame.

Creating a link to a frame is useful when you place a table of contents, navigational tools or search tools in one frame and you want the linked Web pages to appear in another frame.

CREATE A LINK TO A FRAME

1 Select the text or click the image you want readers to select to display a Web page in another frame. To select text, see page 52.

Note: To add an image, see pages 88 to 91.

2 Click 🔗 to create a link.

■ The Create Hyperlink dialog box appears.

■ This area displays all the Web pages in your current Web site.

3 To link the text or image to a Web page in your current Web site, click the Web page in this area.

■ To link the text or image to a page on the Web, click this area and type the address of the Web page.

TIP

What should I consider when creating a link to another frame?

Make sure the text or image you use for a link clearly indicates where the link will take your readers. Do not use the phrase "Click Here" for a link, since this phrase is not very informative.

TIP

When a reader selects a link, which frame will display the linked Web page?

When you create frames, FrontPage will automatically set up one frame to display links and another frame that will display the linked Web pages. In most cases, linked Web pages will appear in the largest frame.

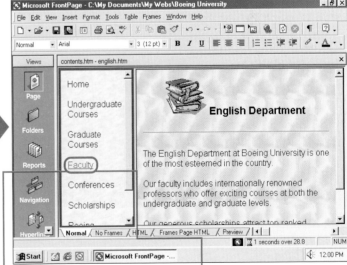

4 Click **OK** to create the link.

■ FrontPage creates the link. Text links appear underlined and in color.

■ To deselect text, click outside the selected area.

■ A reader can click the link to display the linked Web page in another frame.

Note: To test the link, you must use the Preview view. For information on the Preview view, see page 40.

173

CHAPTER 11

CREATE FORMS

Would you like to create forms your readers can use to send you information? Find out how in this chapter.

Forms allow you to gather information from readers who visit your Web pages. You must set up a form before you can add information to the form.

You can create a form that lets readers send you questions or comments about your Web pages. You can also create a form that allows readers to purchase your products and services on the Web.

SET UP A FORM

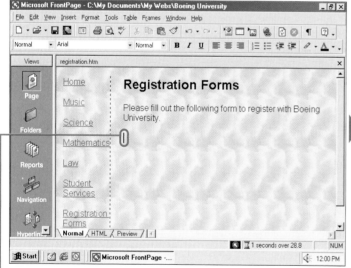

1 Click the location where you want the form to appear on your Web page.

2 Click **Insert**.

3 Click **Form**.

4 Click **Form**.

Note: If Form does not appear on the menu, position the mouse over the bottom of the menu to display all the menu commands.

What should I consider before I set up a form on my Web page?

Before you set up a form on your Web page, make sure FrontPage Server Extensions are installed on your Web server. You can determine if your Web server uses FrontPage Server Extensions by asking the company that will make your Web pages available on the Web.

How do forms work?

A reader can enter information and select options on a form. When a reader clicks the Submit button, the information transfers to your Web server.

When your Web server receives information from a form, the server processes the information. By default, the results of a form are stored in a text file on your Web server. To change how you access the results of a form, see page 190.

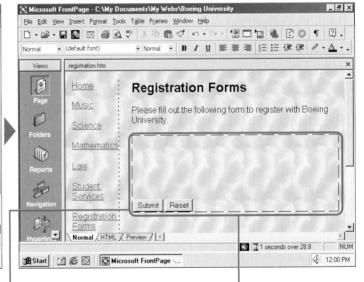

■ The form appears on your Web page. A dashed outline shows the boundaries of the form.

■ The Submit and Reset buttons automatically appear in the form.

■ When a reader clicks the Submit button, the information entered in the form will transfer to your Web server.

■ When a reader clicks the Reset button, the information entered in the form will disappear and the form will display its original settings.

5 To increase the size of the form so you can easily add information to the form, press the Enter key several times.

■ You can now add information to the form. To add information to a form, see pages 178 to 189.

■ To delete a form, position the mouse I to the left of the form (I changes to ⇗) and then double-click to select the form. Then press the Delete key.

You can add a one-line text box that allows readers to enter a line of text.

One-line text boxes are commonly used for entering names and addresses.

ADD A ONE-LINE TEXT BOX

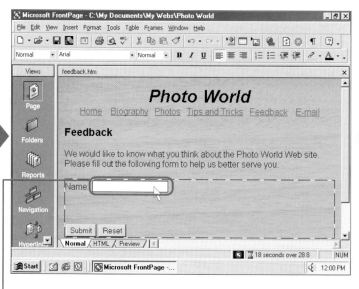

1 Click the area on your form where you want to add a one-line text box.

2 Type the text you want to appear beside the text box. Then press the **Spacebar** to add a blank space.

3 Click **Insert**.

4 Click **Form**.

5 Click **One-Line Text Box**.

■ The text box appears on your Web page.

6 Double-click the text box to change the properties of the text box.

■ The Text Box Properties dialog box appears.

Can I create a one-line text box that hides information that readers enter?

You can create a one-line text box that displays an asterisk (*) for each character a reader types. This is known as a password box. A password box lets readers enter confidential information, such as a password or credit card number, without other people viewing the information. To create a password box, click **Yes** beside Password field in the Text Box Properties dialog box (○ changes to ⊙).

Will the width of a one-line text box affect the number of characters readers can enter in the text box?

No. The width of a text box only determines the size of the text box on your Web page. If readers enter more characters than the text box can display, the existing text moves to the left to make room for the new text.

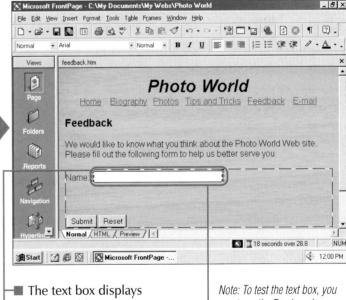

7 Type a name for the text box. A name should not contain blank spaces.

Note: The name you enter will not appear on your Web page. The name helps you identify the information readers enter in the text box when you view the form results.

8 To change the width of the text box, double-click this area and type the width you want to use in characters.

9 Click **OK**.

■ The text box displays the new width.

■ A reader can click in the text box and type the requested information.

Note: To test the text box, you must use the Preview view. For information on the Preview view, see page 40.

■ To delete a one-line text box, click the text box and then press the Delete key.

You can add a scrolling text box that allows readers to enter several lines or paragraphs of text.

A scrolling text box is ideal for gathering comments or questions from your readers.

ADD A SCROLLING TEXT BOX

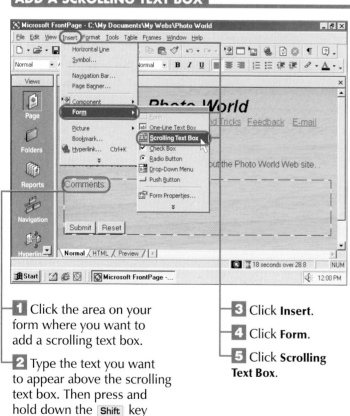

1 Click the area on your form where you want to add a scrolling text box.

2 Type the text you want to appear above the scrolling text box. Then press and hold down the Shift key as you press the Enter key to start a new line.

3 Click **Insert**.

4 Click **Form**.

5 Click **Scrolling Text Box**.

■ The scrolling text box appears on your Web page.

6 Double-click the scrolling text box to change the properties of the text box.

■ The Scrolling Text Box Properties dialog box appears.

TIP

Can I change the size of a scrolling text box?

You can change the size of a scrolling text box as you would change the size of an image on your Web page. When you change the size of a scrolling text box, you should make sure the text box will clearly display the text readers type. If the text readers type does not fit in the text box, readers can use the scroll bar to scroll through the text. To change the size of an image, see page 93.

7 Type a name for the scrolling text box. A name should not contain blank spaces.

Note: The name you enter will not appear on your Web page. The name helps you identify the information readers enter in the text box when you view the form results.

8 Click **OK**.

■ A reader can click in the scrolling text box and type the requested information.

Note: To test the scrolling text box, you must use the Preview view. For information on the Preview view, see page 40.

■ To delete a scrolling text box, click the text box and then press the Delete key.

Which of the following states
have you visited?

☑ California   ☑ Florida

☑ New York   ☐ Arizona

☐ Texas   ☑ Ohio

You can include check boxes on a form if you want readers to be able to select one or more options.

ADD CHECK BOXES

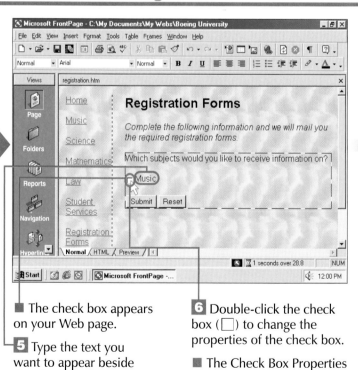

1 Click the area on your form where you want to add a check box.

2 Click **Insert**.

3 Click **Form**.

4 Click **Check Box**.

■ The check box appears on your Web page.

5 Type the text you want to appear beside the check box.

6 Double-click the check box (☐) to change the properties of the check box.

■ The Check Box Properties dialog box appears.

TIP

What information do I need to specify when creating check boxes?

Name

You need to specify a name that describes the check box. The name identifies the check box when you view the results of the form.

Value

You need to specify a value for the check box. When you view the results of the form, the value appears with the name of the check box to indicate the check box was selected.

Initial state

You need to specify if you want the check box to appear checked or not checked on your form. If most people will select the option, you should choose to have the check box appear checked.

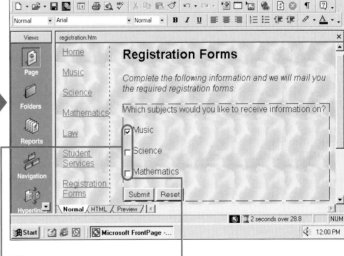

7 Type a name for the check box. A name should not contain blank spaces.

8 Double-click this area and type a value for the check box.

Note: The name and value you enter will not appear on your Web page.

9 If you want the check box to appear automatically selected, click **Checked** (○ changes to ⊙).

10 Click **OK**.

11 You can repeat steps **1** to **10** for each check box you want to add.

■ A reader can click the check box for each option they want to select (□ changes to ☑).

Note: To test the check box, you must use the Preview view. For information on the Preview view, see page 40.

■ To delete a check box, click the check box (□) and then press the Delete key.

You can include a group of radio buttons on a form if you want readers to select only one of several options.

What is your sex?
● Male ○ Female

How old are you?
○ Under 21 ● 21-29 ○ 30-39 ○ Over 40

Where do you live?
● California ○ Arizona ○ Washington
○ New Mexico ○ Florida ○ Other

What is your salary range?
○ Under $20,000 ○ $20,000-$35,000
○ $36,000-$50,000 ● Over $50,000

Submit Reset

ADD RADIO BUTTONS

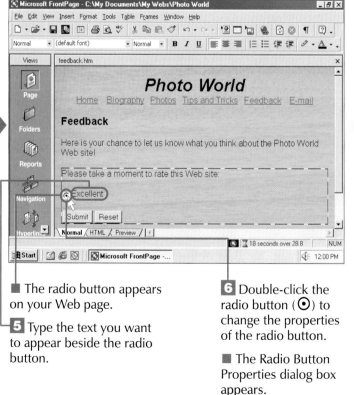

1 Click the area on your form where you want to add the first radio button.

2 Click **Insert**.

3 Click **Form**.

4 Click **Radio Button**.

■ The radio button appears on your Web page.

5 Type the text you want to appear beside the radio button.

6 Double-click the radio button (●) to change the properties of the radio button.

■ The Radio Button Properties dialog box appears.

What information do I need to specify when creating radio buttons?

Group name="age"

Value="thirties"

Initial state="Selected"

Group name

You need to specify a name that describes the group of radio buttons. The name identifies the group of radio buttons when you view the results of the form.

Value

You need to specify a value that describes each radio button. The value identifies the selected radio button when you view the results of the form.

Initial state

You need to specify if you want a radio button to appear selected or not selected on your form. Only one radio button in a group can appear selected.

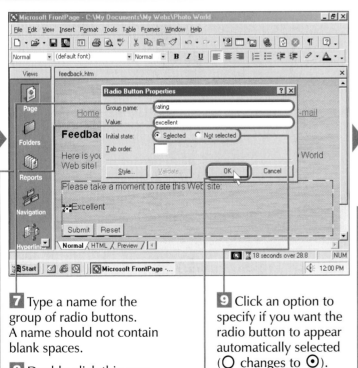

7 Type a name for the group of radio buttons. A name should not contain blank spaces.

8 Double-click this area and type a value for the radio button.

Note: The name and value you enter will not appear on your Web page.

9 Click an option to specify if you want the radio button to appear automatically selected (○ changes to ⊙).

10 Click **OK**.

11 You can repeat steps 1 to 10 for each radio button you want to add.

■ A reader can click a radio button to select one of several options (○ changes to ⊙).

Note: To test the radio button, you must use the Preview view. For information on the Preview view, see page 40.

■ To delete a radio button, click the radio button (○) and then press the Delete key.

You can add a drop-down menu to provide a list of items that readers can choose from.

Please select your age:

Under 25 ▼

Under 25
26-39
40-60
Over 60

Drop-down menus are commonly used for displaying lists of age groups, states and products.

ADD A DROP-DOWN MENU

1 Click the area on your form where you want to add a drop-down menu.

2 Type the text you want to appear beside the drop-down menu. Then press the **Spacebar** to add a blank space.

3 Click **Insert**.

4 Click **Form**.

5 Click **Drop-Down Menu**.

■ The drop-down menu appears on your Web page. The menu appears empty.

6 Double-click the drop-down menu to add items to the menu.

■ The Drop-Down Menu Properties dialog box appears.

What information do I need to specify when creating a drop-down menu?

Name

You need to specify a name that describes the drop-down menu. The name identifies the drop-down menu when you view the results of the form.

Choice

You need to specify the text you want to appear for each item in the drop-down menu.

Value

You can specify a value for each item in the drop-down menu. When you view the results of the form, the value identifies the menu item a reader selected. The value can be the same as the text displayed in the menu or you can use different text. For example, you can use a more specific or shorter name, such as CA for California.

7 Type a name to describe the drop-down menu. A name should not contain blank spaces.

Note: The name you enter will not appear on your Web page. The name helps you identify the drop-down menu when you view the form results.

8 Click **Add** to add an item to the drop-down menu.

■ The Add Choice dialog box appears.

9 Type the first item you want to appear in the menu.

10 To specify a value for the item, click **Specify Value** (☐ changes to ☑).

■ By default, the text you typed in step **9** appears as the value.

11 To use a different value, drag the mouse I over the text in this area until you highlight all the text. Then type the value you want to use.

CONTINUED

You can have a drop-down menu item appear automatically selected on your form. This is useful if most people will select the item.

ADD A DROP-DOWN MENU (CONTINUED)

12 If you want the menu item to appear automatically selected, click **Selected** (○ changes to ⊙). You can have only one menu item appear automatically selected.

13 Click **OK** to add the menu item.

■ You can repeat steps **8** to **13** for each item you want to add to the drop-down menu.

■ Each menu item you add appears in this area.

TIP

Why would I change the number of items readers initially see in a drop-down menu?

To save space on your form, FrontPage initially sets up a drop-down menu to show only the first item in the menu. Readers can click the arrow ▼ to display all the menu items.

If you have a short list of items, you may want a drop-down menu to display all the items. For example, if your drop-down menu contains three items, you can set the height at 3 to display all three items on your form.

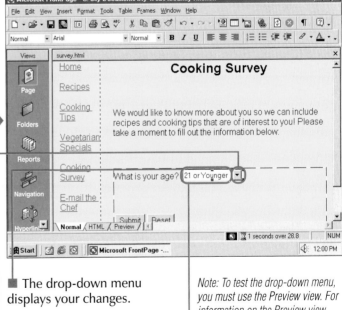

■ This area displays the number of items that readers will initially see in the drop-down menu.

14 To change the number of items that readers will initially see, double-click this area and type a new number.

15 Click **OK** to confirm all of your changes.

■ The drop-down menu displays your changes.

■ A reader can click the arrow ▼ to display the menu items.

Note: To test the drop-down menu, you must use the Preview view. For information on the Preview view, see page 40.

■ To delete a drop-down menu, click the menu and then press the Delete key.

After you create a form, you need to specify how you want to access the results of the form.

ACCESS FORM RESULTS

1 To specify how you want to access the results of a form, click anywhere in the form.

2 Click **Insert**.

3 Click **Form**.

4 Click **Form Properties**.

■ The Form Properties dialog box appears.

■ This area displays the location and name of the file on your Web server where the results of your form will be stored.

■ If you do not want to store the results of the form in a file on your Web server, drag the mouse I over the text in this area until you highlight all the information. Then press the Delete key to remove the information.

How can I access the results of a form?

Store form results in a file on the Web server

You can store the form results in a file on the Web server that stores your Web pages. When a reader enters information into a form, the information will be added to the file.

Send form results in an e-mail message

You can send the form results in an e-mail message addressed to you. When a reader enters information into a form, the information will be sent to your e-mail address. To use this feature, your Web server must be set up to send the results of forms in e-mail messages.

5 To send the results of the form in an e-mail message, click this area and then type your e-mail address.

Note: You can store the results of the form in a file on your Web server as well as send the results of the form in an e-mail message.

6 Click **Options** if you want to change the options for the file stored on your Web server or an e-mail message containing the form results.

■ The Options for Saving Results of Form dialog box appears.

CONTINUED

If you will access the results of the form from a file on your Web server, you can choose a format for the file.

You should choose a file format based on the way you plan to use the form results. HTML file formats are useful if you want to view the information on the Web. The other formats are useful if you plan to use the form results in a spreadsheet or database program.

ACCESS FORM RESULTS (CONTINUED)

7 Click this area to display a list of the available file formats.

8 Click the file format you want to use.

9 If you selected an HTML option in step **8**, drag the mouse I over the **txt** extension in this area until you select the text. Then type the **htm** extension.

Note: Changing the file extension from txt to htm allows Web browsers to properly display the file containing the form results.

10 Click the **E-mail Results** tab if you want to change the options for sending the form results in an e-mail message.

11 Click this area and type the subject you want to display for each e-mail message you receive.

12 Click **OK**.

TIP

How do I view the results of a form on my Web server?

You can view the results of a form in your Web browser. FrontPage stores the results of the form in the _private folder, which is a hidden folder on your Web server. Readers browsing through your Web pages cannot view the contents of this folder.

You will need to enter your user name and password supplied by your Web presence provider to access the form results.

1 Click this area and type the address of the Web server where you published your Web pages followed by **/_private/form_results.txt** or **/_private/form_results.htm**. The file name you type depends on whether you changed the file name in step **9**.

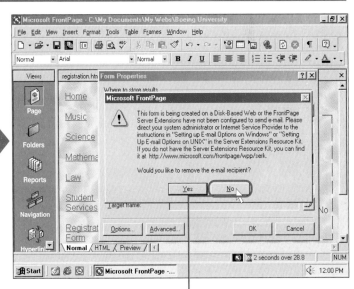

13 Click **OK** to confirm all your changes.

■ If you entered an e-mail address in step **5**, a dialog box appears, stating that your computer is not set up to send the results of your form in an e-mail message.

Note: This dialog box only applies to people who will use their own computer to publish their Web pages. If you are using a Web presence provider to publish your Web pages, you can ignore this message.

14 Click **No** to keep the e-mail address you specified.

CHAPTER 12

MANAGE WEB PAGES

Would you like to keep track of your Web site's progress? This chapter shows you how to create and work with tasks, use reports and more.

> You can create a to-do list to keep track of Web pages you need to work on.

You can add a task to remind you to add, update, review or confirm information on a Web page at a later time.

You can associate each task you add with a specific Web page.

ADD A TASK

1 Click **Folders** to display a list of all the Web pages in your Web site.

■ This area displays the Web pages ( ) and images ( ) in your Web site.

2 Click the Web page you want to associate with a task.

3 Click in this area.

4 Click **Task**.

Can I add a task that is not associated with a specific Web page?

Yes. This is useful if you have a task that relates to more than one Web page, such as a task for verifying all of the phone numbers that appear on your Web pages.

To add a task that is not associated with a specific Web page, click the **Tasks** icon and then perform steps **3** to **8** below.

■ The New Task dialog box appears.

5 Type a name for the task.

6 Click a priority for the task (○ changes to ⊙).

■ This area displays the file name of the Web page associated with the task.

7 Click this area and type a description for the task.

8 Click **OK** to add the task.

■ You can repeat steps **2** to **8** for each task you want to add.

Note: To view your tasks, see page 198.

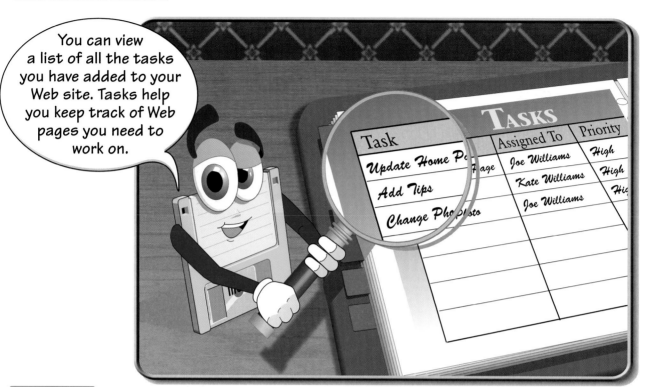

You can view a list of all the tasks you have added to your Web site. Tasks help you keep track of Web pages you need to work on.

VIEW TASKS

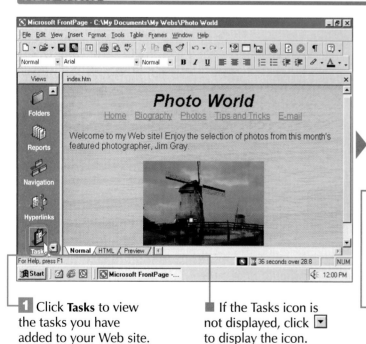

1 Click **Tasks** to view the tasks you have added to your Web site.

■ If the Tasks icon is not displayed, click ▼ to display the icon.

■ This area displays information about each task, such as the name, priority and Web page associated with the task.

■ To view the tasks in a different order, click the heading of the column you want to use to sort the tasks.

Note: You can click the heading of the column again to sort the tasks in the opposite order.

You can change the information you specified for a task, such as providing a more accurate name or more detailed description for the task.

EDIT A TASK

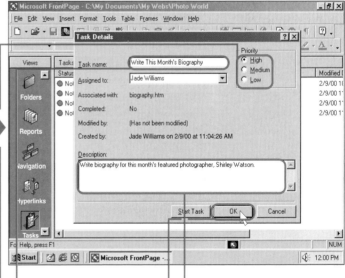

1 Click **Tasks** to view the tasks you have added to your Web site.

2 Double-click the task you want to change.

■ The Task Details dialog box appears.

3 To change the name of the task, type a new name.

4 To change the priority of the task, click a different priority (○ changes to ⊙).

5 To change the description of the task, drag the mouse I over the existing text until you highlight the text. Then type a new description.

6 Click **OK** to save your changes.

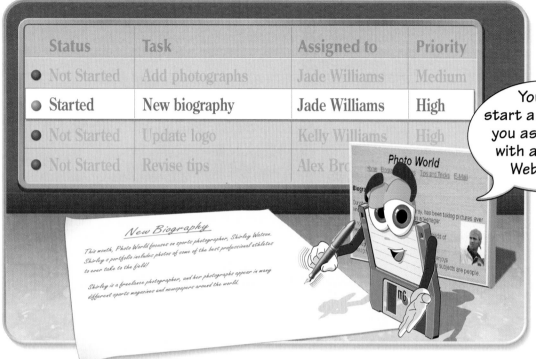

You can start a task that you associated with a specific Web page.

You cannot start a task that you did not associate with a specific Web page.

START A TASK

1 Click **Tasks** to view the tasks you have added to your Web site.

■ This column displays the Web page you associated with each task.

Note: If an area is blank, you did not associate the task with a Web page.

2 Right-click the task you want to start. A menu appears.

3 Click **Start Task**.

■ The Web page associated with the task appears in the Page view.

■ You can now work on the task.

You can delete a task you have completed to keep your list of tasks up to date.

DELETE A TASK

1 Click **Tasks** to view the tasks you have added to your Web site.

2 Click the task you want to delete.

3 Press the Delete key to delete the task.

■ A confirmation dialog box appears.

4 Click **Yes** to delete the task.

■ The task disappears from the list of tasks.

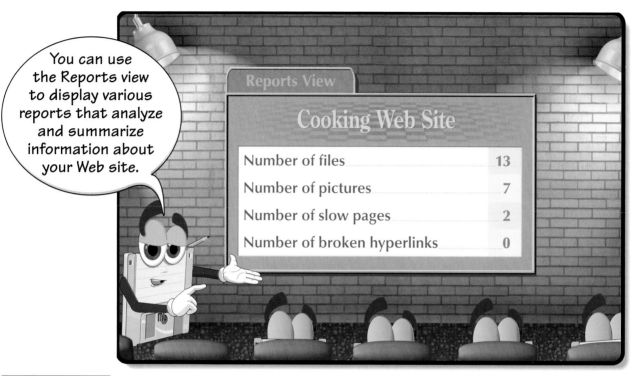

You can use the Reports view to display various reports that analyze and summarize information about your Web site.

USING REPORTS

1 Click **Reports**.

■ The Site Summary report appears in this area. This report provides an overview of your Web site, including the total size of all the files in the Web site and the total number of images in the Web site.

2 To display a different report, click this area.

Note: If the Reporting toolbar is not displayed, see page 16 to display the toolbar.

3 Click the report you want to display.

Note: You may need to scroll through the list to find the report you want to display.

TIP

What reports does FrontPage offer?

Here are some reports that FrontPage offers to help you review and analyze the information in your Web site.

Report	Description
Site Summary	Provides an overview of your Web site.
All Files	Displays information about each file in your Web site.
Recently Added Files	Displays files created in the last 30 days.
Recently Changed Files	Displays files changed in the last 30 days.
Older Files	Displays files you have not changed in the last 72 days.
Unlinked Files	Displays files you cannot access from your home page.
Slow Pages	Displays Web pages that may take at least 1 second to download when using a 28.8 Kb/s modem.
Broken Hyperlinks	Displays the status of the links in your Web site.

■ FrontPage displays the report you selected.

■ In this example, the Recently Added Files report appears. This report shows information about the files you created in the last 30 days.

■ This area displays the name of the report.

■ To view the files in a different order, click the heading of the column you want to use to sort the files.

Note: You can click the heading of the column again to sort the files in the opposite order.

You can add a hit counter to your Web page to keep track of the number of people who have visited the page.

A hit counter displays the number of times a Web page has been viewed. For example, a hit counter will display "50" if one person displays the Web page 50 times or if 50 people view the Web page once.

ADD A HIT COUNTER

1 Click the location where you want to add a hit counter to your Web page.

2 Click 🔲 to display a list of components that you can add to your Web page.

3 Click **Hit Counter**.

■ The Hit Counter Properties dialog box appears.

4 Click the style of hit counter you want to use (○ changes to ⊙).

■ When you add a hit counter to your Web page, the hit counter automatically starts at zero.

5 To start the hit counter at a specific number, click this option (☐ changes to ✔).

6 Double-click this area and type the starting number you want to use.

TIP

What should I consider before adding a hit counter to my Web page?

To use a hit counter, your Web server must use FrontPage Server Extensions. You can determine if your Web server uses FrontPage Server Extensions by asking the company that will make your Web pages available on the Web.

TIP

Which Web page should I add a hit counter to?

Most people add a hit counter to their home page since this is the first page people will see when they visit the Web site. The home page is named index.htm. You can also add hit counters to other Web pages to determine which pages are the most popular.

7 Click **OK** to create the hit counter.

■ The text **[Hit Counter]** appears on your Web page.

■ The hit counter will replace the text when you publish the Web page.

Note: You must publish your Web page before you can view a hit counter.

■ To remove a hit counter, click **[Hit Counter]** and then press the Delete key.

CHAPTER 13

PUBLISH WEB PAGES

Are you ready to publish your Web pages? Learn how in this chapter.

Web presence providers are companies that store Web pages and make them available on the Web.

Web presence providers store Web pages on computers called Web servers. Web servers store, monitor and control access to Web pages.

INTERNET SERVICE PROVIDERS

Internet service providers are companies that offer people access to the Internet. Most Internet service providers offer space on their Web servers where customers can publish their Web pages free of charge.

COMMERCIAL ONLINE SERVICES

Commercial online services such as America Online will publish Web pages created by customers for free. Many commercial online services offer easy-to-use programs to help people create and publish Web pages.

FREE WEB PRESENCE PROVIDERS

Many companies on the Web will publish your Web pages for free. These companies offer a limited amount of storage space and may place advertisements on your Web pages.

You can find companies that will publish your Web pages for free at the following Web sites:

geocities.yahoo.com

www.tripod.lycos.com

xoom.com

DEDICATED WEB PRESENCE PROVIDERS

Dedicated Web presence providers are companies that specialize in publishing Web pages for a fee. Dedicated Web presence providers are flexible and offer features that other Web presence providers do not offer.

You can find dedicated Web presence providers at the following Web sites:

www.dreamhost.com

www.hostess.com

www.pair.com

YOUR OWN WEB SERVER

Purchasing your own Web server is the most expensive way to publish Web pages and requires a full-time connection to the Internet. Setting up and maintaining your own Web server is difficult but will give you the greatest amount of control over your Web pages.

CHOOSE A WEB PRESENCE PROVIDER

You should consider several factors when choosing a Web presence provider to publish your Web pages.

TECHNICAL SUPPORT

A Web presence provider should have a technical support department to answer your questions. You should be able to contact the department by telephone or e-mail. A good technical support department will respond to questions you send by e-mail within a day.

TRAFFIC LIMIT

When readers view your Web pages, information transfers from the Web server to their computers. The amount of information that transfers depends on the number of people that view your Web pages and the file size of your pages.

Most Web presence providers limit the amount of information that can transfer in one day. If more information transfers, you may have to pay extra. You should choose a Web presence provider that allows at least 50 MB (megabytes) of information to transfer in one day.

RELIABILITY

Make sure the Web presence provider you choose is reliable. A Web presence provider should be able to tell you how often their Web servers shut down. You may want to ask a Web presence provider for customer references that you can contact. You should take into consideration that all Web presence providers occasionally shut down their Web servers for maintenance and upgrades.

XYZ Web Server Reliability

2% Downtime

STORAGE SPACE

Most Web presence providers limit the amount of space you can use to store your Web pages. Choose a Web presence provider that allows you to store at least 5 MB (megabytes) of information.

ACCESS LOGS

A good Web presence provider will supply you with statistics about your Web pages, such as which Web pages are the most popular and where your readers are from. You may also be able to view any error messages readers may see when viewing your Web pages, such as "Page Not Found." Access logs can help you determine if you need to make changes to your Web pages.

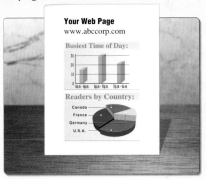

DOMAIN NAME REGISTRATION

For a fee, you can choose the address, or domain name, that people type to access your Web pages. A personalized domain name is easy for people to remember and will not change if you switch to another Web presence provider. Most Web presence providers will register your domain name for a fee.

FRONTPAGE SERVER EXTENSIONS

Your Web presence provider must have FrontPage Server Extensions installed on their Web server for some advanced Web page features to work. For example, you will need FrontPage Server Extensions to use forms and some components, such as hit counters, on your Web pages.

You can specify keywords to help search tools catalog your Web pages.

Search tools help people find Web pages that discuss information of interest. Popular search tools include AltaVista, Lycos and Yahoo!.

When readers enter words in a search tool that match your keywords, your Web page will more likely appear in the search results.

SPECIFY KEYWORDS FOR WEB PAGES

1 Click **File**.

2 Click **Properties**.

Note: If Properties does not appear on the menu, position the mouse ⌖ over the bottom of the menu to display all the menu commands.

■ The Page Properties dialog box appears.

3 Click the **Custom** tab.

4 Click **Add** to specify keywords for your Web page.

TIP

Will the keywords I entered appear on my Web page?

Readers will not see the keywords you entered when viewing your Web page. Keywords appear in the HTML code for the Web page. To view the HTML code for a Web page, see page 40.

sales, invoices, information

TIP

What words should I specify as keywords?

You should use both general and specific words to describe your Web page. For example, if your Web page contains information about corvettes, use the keywords "car" and "corvette." You may also want to include misspelled words that people may type, such as "corvete."

■ The User Meta Variable dialog box appears.

5 Type **keywords** to specify that you want to define keywords for your Web page.

6 Click this area and type the keywords you want to use, separated by commas.

7 Click **OK** to confirm the keywords you entered.

■ The keywords you entered appear in this area.

■ To change the keywords, double-click the keywords and then repeat steps 6 and 7.

8 Click **OK** to close the Page Properties dialog box.

When you finish creating your Web pages, you can transfer the pages to a Web server to make the pages available on the Web.

Before you can transfer your Web pages to a Web server, you must choose a Web presence provider that will publish your Web pages. For information on Web presence providers, see pages 208 to 211.

TRANSFER WEB PAGES TO WEB SERVER

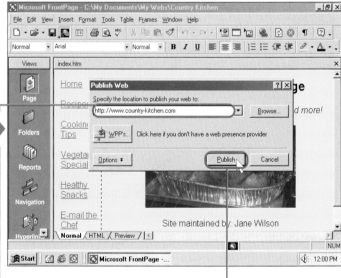

■ You need to connect to the Internet before you can transfer your Web pages to a Web server.

1 Click 🖫 to publish your Web pages.

■ The Publish Web dialog box appears.

2 Click this area and type the address of the Web server where you want to publish your Web pages.

3 Click **Publish**.

What information do I need to transfer my Web pages to a Web server?

You will need the following information to transfer your Web pages to a Web server. If you do not know the information, ask your Web presence provider.

Web server address

User name

Password

How do I update my Web pages on the Web server?

If you make changes to Web pages on your computer, you must transfer the updated pages to the Web server. The updated Web pages will replace the old Web pages on the Web server. To transfer the updated Web pages to the Web server, click .

■ A dialog box appears, asking for your user name and password.

4 Type your user name.

5 Click this area and type your password.

Note: A symbol (ˣ) appears for each character you type to prevent others from seeing your password.

6 Click **OK**.

■ FrontPage copies your Web pages to the Web server.

■ This message appears when your Web pages have been published successfully.

■ You can click this option to view your published Web pages on the Web.

7 Click **Done** to close the dialog box.

After you publish your Web pages, there are several ways you can let people know about the pages.

MAIL ANNOUNCEMENTS

You can mail an announcement about your Web pages to family, friends, colleagues and clients. You can also mail information about your Web pages to local newspapers and magazines that may be interested in your Web pages.

E-MAIL MESSAGES

Most e-mail programs include a feature, called a signature, that allows you to add the same information to the end of every e-mail message you send. You can use a signature to include information about your Web pages in all your e-mail messages.

EXCHANGE LINKS

If another page on the Web discusses ideas related to your Web pages, you can ask the author to include a link to your pages if you do the same. This allows people reading the other Web page to easily visit your Web pages.

WEB PAGE ADVERTISEMENTS

Many companies set aside areas on their Web pages where you can advertise your Web pages. You can use the LinkExchange to advertise your Web pages free of charge. The LinkExchange is located at the adnetwork.bcentral.com Web site.

NEWSGROUPS

You can send an announcement about your Web pages to discussion groups on the Internet called newsgroups. Make sure you choose newsgroups that discuss topics related to your Web pages. You can announce new or updated Web pages to the comp.infosystems.www.announce newsgroup.

MAILING LISTS

You can send an announcement to carefully selected mailing lists on the Internet. A mailing list is a discussion group that communicates through e-mail. You should read the messages in a mailing list for a week before sending an announcement to make sure the mailing list members would be interested in your Web pages. You can find a directory of mailing lists at the www.liszt.com Web site.

SEARCH TOOLS

Search tools help people quickly find information on the Web. You can add your Web pages to various search tools so people can easily find your Web pages. Some popular search tools include:

AltaVista	www.altavista.com
Lycos	www.lycos.com
Yahoo!	www.yahoo.com

You can add your Web pages to many search tools at once at the www.submit-it.com Web site.

INDEX

SIMPLIFIED SERIES

Microsoft Office 2000 Simplified

ISBN 0-7645-6052-2
$29.99 USA/£28.99 UK
$39.99 CAN

Microsoft Word 2000 Simplified

ISBN 0-7645-6054-9
$24.99 USA/£23.99 UK
$32.99 CAN

Microsoft Excel 2000 Simplified

ISBN 0-7645-6053-0
$24.99 USA/£23.99 UK
$32.99 CAN

Microsoft Access 2000 Simplified

ISBN 0-7645-6058-1
$24.99 USA/£23.99 UK
$32.99 CAN

Internet and World Wide Web Simplified, 3rd Edition

ISBN 0-7645-3409-2
$24.99 USA/£23.99 UK
$32.99 CAN

Computers Simplified, 4th Edition

ISBN 0-7645-6042-5
$24.99 USA/£23.99 UK
$32.99 CAN

PC Upgrade and Repair Simplified

ISBN 0-7645-6049-2
$24.99 USA/£23.99 UK
$32.99 CAN

Word For Windows 95 Simplified

ISBN 1-56884-681-9
$19.99 USA/£18.99 UK
$29.99 CAN

Word 6 For Windows Simplified

ISBN 1-56884-660-6
$19.99 USA/£18.99 UK
$29.99 CAN

WordPerfect 6.1 For Windows Simplified

ISBN 1-56884-665-7
$19.99 USA/£18.99 UK
$29.99 CAN

POCKETGUIDES

The Proven 3-D Visual Approach To Learning Computers In A Handy Pocket Size.

Windows 98 Visual PocketGuide

ISBN 0-7645-6035-2
$16.99 USA/£15.99 UK
$23.99 CAN

Windows 95 Visual PocketGuide

ISBN 1-56884-661-4
$14.99 USA/£13.99 UK
$21.99 CAN

ALSO AVAILABLE:

Windows 3.1 Visual PocketGuide

ISBN 1-56884-650-9
$14.99 USA/£13.99 UK
$21.99 CAN

 ...Visit our Web site at www.maran.com